Radio Free Europe

ADST-DACOR Diplomats and Diplomacy Series

Series Editor: Margery Boichel Thompson

Since 1776, extraordinary men and women have represented the United States abroad under all sorts of circumstances. What they did and how and why they did it remain little known to their compatriots. In 1995 the Association for Diplomatic Studies and Training (ADST) and DACOR, an organization of foreign affairs professionals, created the Diplomats and Diplomacy book series to increase public knowledge and appreciation of the role of diplomats in world history. The series seeks to demystify diplomacy through the stories of those who have conducted foreign relations, as they lived, influenced, and reported them. Jim Brown's *Radio Free Europe: An Insider's View*, the 53rd volume in the series, tells the story of the critical role communications played throughout the Cold War.

Related Titles in the Series

Wilson P. Dizard, *Inventing Public Diplomacy: The Story of the United States Information Agency*

Robert William Farrand, *Reconstruction and Peace Building in the Balkans: The Brčko Experience*

James E. Goodby, Dmitri Trenin, and Petrus Buwalda, with Yves Pagniez, *A Strategy for Stable Peace: Towards a Euroatlantic Security Community*

Brandon Grove, *Behind Embassy Walls: The Life and Times of an American Diplomat*

Paul Hacker, *Slovakia on the Road to Independence: An American Diplomat's Eyewitness Account*

Robert V. Keeley, *The Colonels' Coup and the American Embassy: A Diplomat's View of the Breakdown of Democracy in Cold War Greece*

Kempton Jenkins, *Cold War Saga*

Bo Lidegaard, *Defiant Diplomacy: Henrik Kauffmann, Denmark, and the United States in World War II and the Cold War 1939-1958*

David D. Newsom, *Witness to a Changing World*

Yale Richmond, *Practicing Public Diplomacy: A Cold War Odyssey*

For a complete list of series titles visit www.adst.org/publications

Radio Free Europe
An Insider's View

J. F. Brown

Foreword by A. Ross Johnson

An ADST-DACOR Diplomats and Diplomacy Book

NAP NEW ACADEMIA PUBLISHING VELLUM

Washington, DC

Printed in the United States of America

Library of Congress Control Number: 2013948495
ISBN 978-0-9886376-8-9 paperback (alk. paper)

VELLUM   An imprint of New Academia Publishing

NAP NEW ACADEMIA PUBLISHING   New Academia Publishing
PO Box 27420, Washington, DC 20038-7420
info@newacademia.com - www.newacademia.com

To Dick Rowson

Contents

Foreword

A. Ross Johnson

"A communist country could only exist by means of lies and lack of information. Communism could be torn apart, not by power of arms, but by power of words and belief—genuine belief. That is why Radio Free Europe has been more important than the armies, the missiles. . . . This was Washington's most important investment during the Cold War." This was the conclusion of Romanian president Emil Constantinescu, visiting Radio Free Europe/Radio Liberty in Prague in 1997.

His views were widely shared by post-1989 democratic leaders in Eastern Europe. Asked if Radio Free Europe had contributed to the victory of the Solidarity trade union in Poland, Lech Wałęsa replied, "Would the earth exist without the sun?" Or, as Jim Brown says in this book about meeting President Václav Havel in the Prague Castle: "I was introduced as a former director of Radio Free Europe; Havel looked at me, smiled, and said 'Jim! We were colleagues!' That made everything worthwhile."

Havel later characterized RFE's influence and significance as "great and profound." His words were included in video greetings to a 2004 conference at the Hoover Institution on the impact of RFE and Radio Liberty (which broadcast to the Soviet Union). The conference papers and translated documents from Communist-era archives were published in a volume I co-edited with R. Eugene Parta, *Cold War Broadcasting: Impact on the Soviet Union and Eastern Europe* (Central European University Press, 2010). Jim Brown was an active participant in that conference. I hoped he would contribute a chapter to the conference volume, but he was focused on writing his own history of RFE.

Following Jim's death in 2009, Dick Rowson (publisher of many of Jim's books on Eastern Europe at Duke University Press) and I, in cooperation with Margaret Brown, sought a publisher for Jim's manuscript. We are pleased that the work will be published through the good offices of the Association for Diplomatic Studies and Training (ADST), with support from the Freedom Broadcasting Foundation. We have corrected a few names and dates, made one deletion in response to a reviewer's suggestion, and supplied a few explanatory footnotes; but we have not otherwise altered the manuscript, while allowing for the usual copyediting by ADST.

Jim Brown, colleague and friend, was a widely recognized expert on Eastern Europe during the Cold War. He published six books, a number of studies for the RAND Corporation and other research organizations, and many articles. He was regularly consulted by almost all Western journalists reporting on Eastern Europe and participated as a highly respected expert and scholar on Eastern Europe in many international meetings in Europe and the United States. His expertise derived from his service at Radio Free Europe, where he began as a copy editor in 1959 and retired as director in 1983. He returned to Munich in 1992–1993 as senior fellow at the RFE/RL Research Institute, where he wrote *Hopes and Shadows: Eastern Europe after Communism* (Duke University Press, 1994).

Jim Brown had written about Eastern Europe from RFE, but never about RFE—until he wrote this book. Here, as Jim says in his preface, he offers a veteran "'insider's' view of what it was like to be part of a radio that was communicating with nations, European nations, that had been deprived of their freedom." He conveys his understanding of how Radio Free Europe functioned as a decentralized organization that empowered exiles, while also conveying what it, and they, could—and could not––offer East European listeners. Jim Brown's explanations of the function of the central news department as an internal news agency, of discussions with and trust of exile broadcast chiefs, of RFE's cautious approach to broadcasting to Poland under martial law after 1981—to cite only three examples from the book—illuminate the editorial policies and internal relationships that made RFE a success. His portraits of key personalities over the years help us understand that RFE was not just an institution; it was a unique multinational group of people.

The reader will find additional information and perspectives on the issues discussed in this volume in other books by authors who worked at RFE, including Arch Puddington's *Broadcasting Freedom: The Cold War Triumph of Radio Free Europe and Radio Liberty* (University Press of Kentucky, 2000); George R. Urban's *Radio Free Europe and the Pursuit of Democracy: My War within the Cold War* (Yale University Press, 1997); and my own book, *Radio Free Europe and Radio Liberty: The CIA Years and Beyond* (Woodrow Wilson Center Press and Stanford University Press, 2010).

Background on Eastern Europe and the challenges faced by RFE in broadcasting to the region is found in Jim's books published with Duke University Press: *Eastern Europe and Communist Rule* (1988); *Surge to Freedom—The End to Communist Rule in Eastern Europe* (1991); *The Grooves of Change—Eastern Europe at the Turn of the Millennium* (2001); and *Hopes and Shadows: Eastern Europe after Communism* (1994). Also valuable is Jim's first book, *The New Eastern Europe* (Praeger, 1966).

In his Epilogue, "Over Too Soon," Jim argued that a "Radio New Europe" could have made an important contribution to postcommunist democratic transition in Eastern Europe. That became RFE/RL's new mission after 1989. Still broadcasting from Munich until 1995, and after that from Prague, RFE aimed (with much-reduced congressional funding) to provide independent information, detached perspectives, and a model of professional journalism for the new democracies of Eastern Europe. That chapter ended with the inclusion of the region in the European Union. Today, RFE/RL reaches twenty-one countries where free media are banned or limited, in twenty-eight languages, with independent news and information aimed at countering authoritarianism and promoting democracy.

A. Ross Johnson
Washington, D.C.
July 2013

Preface

This book is not autobiographical; at least it is not meant to be. It is primarily about Radio Free Europe (RFE), secondarily about my interaction with it.

Why not just about RFE? Because RFE's institutional history, as well as Radio Liberty's, has been covered more than once, most notably by Arch Puddington in his book *Broadcasting Freedom: The Cold War Triumph of Radio Free Europe and Radio Liberty*. But no story of Radio Free Europe has ever been told by anyone who worked at the Radio's operational headquarters in Munich. There has been no "insider's" view of what it was like to be part of a radio that was communicating with nations, European nations, that had been deprived of their freedom.

That explains my part in the story. I worked for RFE in Munich in several capacities for over twenty-six years and got to know it better than most. This gives me the right and perhaps the responsibility to write this book. Sometimes it may indeed seem to be more about me than about RFE, but I think that this personal aspect gives the story a vibrancy and an authentic immediacy that a neutral and neutered survey simply could not. The last thing I intended was an ego trip.

Radio Free Europe played a not inconsiderable role in the Cold War. It had many listeners, but even their approximate numbers could never be estimated. Most were casual listeners; some were avid, even devoted, listeners. What did RFE do for them? It kept them informed. An informed audience was an alert audience. RFE told them what was happening in the world, and it informed and commented on what was happening in their own countries. It broke the communist information monopoly and gave East Europeans the chance to think and judge for themselves. In doing this it helped preserve their dignity. It tried to keep Eastern Europe's societies together while their communist states were bent on destroying them. This was RFE's basic task, and it was a worthy one.

On a more individual, personal level it kept East Europeans company, kept them in touch with the West, analyzing what was good about it but not attempting to hide what was bad, leveling with its audience, not trying to lever it. Several East Europeans whom I met after 1989 stressed that it was this companionable, almost pastoral, function of RFE that helped keep their spirits up and for which they were the most grateful.

Whatever its mistakes, its weaknesses, and its hypocrisies, Radio Free Europe was a worthy institution. Its story is worth telling.

Jim Brown
Oxford, England
2005

Acknowledgments

Margaret, my wife, encouraged me to write this book and bore with me while I was doing it. Julia was sympathetic, as were Holly and Josh. Dick Rowson was strong in help and support. Lynne Fletcher typed the manuscript (I couldn't). This is her second book with me. Her skill, patience, and good humor continue unabated.

1

The Lowest Ebb

"Do you read much poetry?" It was hardly a question I expected to be asked in my first two minutes at Radio Free Europe. It was put to me, not in the Radio proper, but in its reception space just inside the main entrance.

I noticed that my questioner had a book of verse in his hand. I had come in and taken the chair next to his, probably disturbing him. He was American, a nice man and obviously not too hurt by my philistine shrug in response to his question. He was escorted through reception before I could explain this lacuna in my education. The next time I saw him he was behind a desk in the Central News Room. Radio Free Europe, I soon learned, was a place of diverse culture.

This was July 1957 and I was at RFE's portals for two reasons. My presence in Munich was the result of a successful response to an advertisement in the *Manchester Guardian* several months before for a deputy editor of *Historical Abstracts*, an English-language historical journal based in Munich. Almost no sooner had I arrived in Munich than both *Historical Abstracts* and I realized that we had both made a serious mistake. My wife Margaret and I were resigned to returning to England with burdened brow and tails between our legs. But just a few days before we were scheduled to go home we went to a party at the home of the British consul general in Munich to celebrate the Queen's Birthday. There a sympathetic American elicited my hard luck story from me.

"Have you thought of Radio Free Europe," he asked. I had not. I had only heard of Radio Free Europe for the first time in 1954. One of its propaganda balloons, meant to be heading for Eastern Europe, had blown far off course and landed on a Scottish farmer's land in Perthshire. He had its message translated and then wrote an irate letter to the *Manchester Guardian* demanding to know what the devil was going on. (In fairness to Radio Free Europe I should say that the sponsor of this lunatic balloon scheme was a smaller associate organization separate from it.) Later, I heard about RFE during and after the Hungarian Revolution.

My sympathetic American immediately marched me off to meet another American who worked at Radio Free Europe. Then the briefest of conversations was followed by an invitation to come to the Radio next morning to meet the "Head of Information." Hence my presence — a rather nervous one — in RFE's reception.

My nervousness only increased when I met the Head of Information. He was obviously more nervous than I was. I answered three questions, and then he signaled that the interview was over by producing a comb and passing it through his far from plentiful hair. It was apparently his way of ending interviews. I waited briefly in his outer office, and then his secretary took me up to my first Radio job. I then met my first RFE boss, a Scotsman named Iain MacDonald, who in the 1970s covered the early stages of the Conference on Security and Cooperation in Europe. He was to prove a true colleague and a journalist of real analytical ability.

My job was mainly correcting the written English of RFE's East European staff. I certainly improved my own English in doing so, and I met a large number of the staff concerned. It was excellent preparation for my long Cold War career. I was fascinated by the backgrounds of the East European staff, deeply impressed by their basic honesty, and humbled by the breadth of some of their backgrounds.

Radio in Crisis

I soon realized that Radio Free Europe was in deep crisis. It was only just over eight months since the Hungarian Revolution. The attacks on the Radio's mishandling of the revolution—in Germany, Western

Europe generally, and in the United States—were still continuing. There were strong demands in Germany that the Radio leave, in West Europe and in the United States that it be totally discontinued or drastically reformed. Within the Radio itself the Hungarian staff were divided, fearful, and listless. The others shared their sense of foreboding.

What particularly depressed most RFE Hungarians was the widespread criticism of them inside Hungary itself. And among the large number of Hungarians who left their native land when the revolution was put down there was not a good word for the station.

Enemies at the Outset

But it was not long before I realized that, prior to the Hungarian Revolution, in fact right from its earlier beginnings in 1951, RFE had been the object of numerous attacks in both the United States and Western Europe. The attacks had come from right, left, and center. The right was convinced it had too many communists, the left too many fascists, the center too many of each. Fulton Lewis Jr. was its most persistent American tormenter. But, from my days at the University of Michigan in 1951–52, I had always believed that Fulton Lewis's enmity must be a badge of honor. I was therefore not too worried about this. As for some of the other detractors in the United States and Germany, I felt the same about them too. Whatever faults RFE had in those days, at least it stood for something better than most of its enemies.

The attacks on the Polish Service from West German organizations speaking for Germans expelled from Poland, "*die Vertriebenen*," were even exceeded in volume by the attacks on the Czechoslovak Service from Sudeten German expellees. And since these expellees had considerable support in the Bundestag, the West German parliament in Bonn, even more support in the Bavarian parliament in Munich, as well as considerable media support in Bavaria, as a whole these were onslaughts that could not be ignored.

But the Czechoslovak Service also had to stand virulent attacks from the United States. The main target there was Ferdinand Peroutka. Peroutka had been one of the most famous journalists in the history of Czechoslovakia's First Republic, perhaps best remembered for a series of journalistic duels with President Thomas Masaryk in the 1920s. Peroutka was a Social Democrat. That was enough for his American critics. But most RFE Czechs held him in great respect. I remember him striding the Radio corridors in 1960, when he was "imported" from New York to help restore order in a Czechoslovak Service collapsing from petty feuding and mismanagement. Peroutka had by then survived the onslaught of the 1950s. He was now very much the elder statesman, acting the part naturally and impressively.

The Charges over Hungary: How Genuine?

But these charges were as nothing compared with those that inundated the Radio over the 1956 Hungarian Revolution. RFE was accused both of fomenting the revolution and encouraging it to continue by promising the revolutionaries American military help. Most damagingly, these charges originated with the revolutionaries themselves. Psychology can best explain them: scapegoat syndrome! RFE was, after all, an instrument and a symbol of an America on which Hungarian hopes and dreams had centered. American troops were also close at hand in West Germany. RFE, born of the Cold War, was seen as part of the American offensive against Soviet communism and Russian imperialism. During the revolution it undoubtedly had a large and anxious audience. After defeat, this audience irrationally but understandably presented its list of charges.

Objectively there was little to support any of these accusations. But revolutions are not objective: they are intensely subjective. There is no truth about revolutions, just versions. In 1956 people heard what they wanted to hear and then put the most hopeful twist on it. But the charges against a few RFE programs, once the fighting had begun, do carry some weight. There was one rogue program about making Molotov cocktails and one or two about the proximity, though not the intentions, of American troops. But what the Hungarian broadcasters at RFE could be comprehensively criticized for was the excitement, the shrill partisanship, even the near hysteria of some of their presentations. Small wonder that what they did say was wrongly and tragically misconstrued. RFE's broadcasts were misquoted and distorted, and as such they spread like a prairie fire.

This is not an attempt to exonerate Radio Free Europe. Serious mistakes were made, but they were exaggerated for different reasons and from different motives. Any examination of these mistakes must also center on the situation within the radio itself. Was it equipped to meet the biggest crisis in its history? No, it was not. In the Hungarian Service itself the leadership, though not without some intellectual ability, was aged, enfeebled, and ineffective.

Nor was it psychologically prepared for such a crisis. Its members were conditioned by the context of the Cold War that had created Radio Free Europe. Their thinking about the Cold War was being conditioned from many sources, not only within the Hungarian exile community itself, but also by an American administration that was sponsoring Radio Free Europe, which many saw as speaking for it. There was also the feeling that this Cold War would soon be over—a couple of years at the most. Communist rule would be deposed as quickly as it had been imposed. It was American might against a primitive Russian barbarism that was trying to keep down populations superior to it, alien from it, and disdainful of it. Radio Free Europe had only begun operating in 1951. Now in just over five years came the Hungarian Revolution and an almost similar crisis in Poland. Events seemed to be conforming to expectations.

This mentality also largely explains the policy divisions among RFE's Hungarians that the revolution brought to the fore. Many of them were indeed convinced that it was signaling the demise of communism itself. As to the future this meant returning to the past, to precommunist Hungary, hopefully even to pre–Trianon Hungary. The struggle, therefore, of the Imre Nagy revolutionary regime against the Soviets and their local allies was basically irrelevant. Cardinal Mindszenty was the hero for many RFE Hungarians, certainly not the communist Nagy. A reform communism under Nagy, or anybody else, was the last thing they wanted. And for a few hallucinatory days what they wanted was what they thought they could get.

But it was not just RFE's Hungarians who must take the blame for what became a fiasco. The American management should take even more blame, specifically its policy director, William E.

Griffith. There was neither crisis leadership nor policy direction from the center. This may have been because there was none from Washington, caught as ill prepared as Munich was. The role of the American management was a shabby one, and subsequent efforts to explain, excuse, or defend it only added to the shabbiness. Griffith was a brilliant man, although his relentless intellectual posturing often caused irritation and outright derision. He subsequently left the Radio in 1958, became a professor at MIT, a consultant to a medley of American government agencies, and a globetrotting advisor to the *Readers Digest*.

The Polish Contrast

Immediately preceding the crisis caused by the Hungarian Revolution in November 1956 was what became internationally known as the "Polish October." The way RFE managed this crucial episode was totally different from its bungling over Hungary. This was partly because everything moved in its favor. First, the situation there in Poland: all three sides, the Polish, the Russian, and the Polish people, showed statesmanship. The Polish Communist Party was provident enough to recall Władisław Gomułka, disgraced in 1949, to its top position. Stalin had seen Gomułka as a dangerous nationalist, and Gomułka was lucky to survive with his life. This now gave him a strong appeal among even anticommunist Poles. The Polish people showed determination tempered by restraint. As for its leadership, the contrast with Hungary was all too clear. The Poles had Cardinal Wyszyński, the Hungarians Cardinal Mindszenty. The former showed himself a statesman; the latter was always a reactionary cleric. Wyszyński set about arranging a peace-saving *modus vivendi* with Gomułka. It didn't last long, but it was long enough. It saw the immediate crisis out and saved Poland from a Soviet invasion.

Then there was Khrushchev. He originally wanted to avoid invading Hungary, too. But Nagy's declaration of Hungarian neutrality and his withdrawing of Hungary from the Warsaw Pact left Khrushchev no option. Poland, for once, opted for realism, not romanticism, and was saved. Two invasions in two months could have led to World War III. It would certainly have cost Khrushchev his job.

Inside RFE these developments made life much easier for the Polish broadcasters. But it was the leadership of these broadcasters that made the real difference, leadership given by Jan Nowak, the Polish broadcasting director. During his entire RFE career, which ended in 1975, Nowak, a hero of the wartime Polish underground, could sometimes be wrong, even petty, in everyday matters. But when "it counted"—and it certainly counted in 1956—he was a statesman. He was, in fact, the one man in RFE's history with a touch of greatness about him. There was a nervous excitement in the Polish Service broadcasts during the October crisis, but generally it was a cool calm. The service showed strong support for Wyszyński and a quiet respect for Gomułka. The crisis was soon over. The Polish Broadcast Service not only helped to save Radio Free Europe, but it helped save Poland, too.

The Polish Service (and Jan Nowak) had had a kick-start when Colonel Józef Światło, a senior officer of the UB, Poland's security service, deserted to the West in December 1953. Światło was privy to, or had participated in, the worst excesses of this thoroughly Stalinist organization. He seemed also to know everything about Soviet penetration of the UB and the luxurious living of UB officials. He gave a series of interviews to RFE's Polish Service in 1954 that created a sensation in Poland, shook the communist regime, and established RFE's reputation throughout the country. A reputation it never lost! There was considerable opposition within the Polish Service to using a man like Światło, but Nowak, aware of both the political and journalistic opportunity, would have none of it. It was probably Radio Free Europe's greatest ever coup.

A brief note typifying Nowak. He had many admirers in the West, several prominent journalists among them. None admired him more than the journalist and writer David Halberstam, then of the *New York Times*. It was Nowak's streak of nineteenth century Romanticism that really got to Halberstam. When he asked Nowak when he had left Poland, the answer could have been straight out of Mickiewicz: "I never left Poland."

The first decade of Radio Free Europe's history— the first few "cowboy" years, the Polish October, the Hungarian Revolution, ended with a mixed record and a mixed reputation for the Radio. But it had at least survived. Its job now was both to regain and strengthen confidence, internal and external.

Changes and Chances

Staff changes at RFE were only to be expected after 1956. There were important changes in the head offices in both Munich and New York, in the Munich policy directorate, and in the Hungarian Broadcast Service itself. But in all five Broadcast Services a long lean look was leveled at past approaches, methods, and mindsets. The essential changes occurred within the Broadcast Services themselves, and they happened quite quickly. A comparison between RFE's programs in 1957 and those in 1965 show a stark difference. The Hungarian Revolution itself was enough to make RFE's cold warriors less fervent. So was the distinct possibility that they would lose their jobs if they weren't. Good sense and resilience played their parts, too. RFE was responding and maturing.

One new appointment deserves special mention: that of István Bede as Hungarian Broadcast Service director. Bede had been Hungary's ambassador in London before the communist takeover. As service director for some fifteen years, he tended sometimes to use backstage diplomacy when up-front directness would have been better. But he brought high intelligence, political *nous,* and personal presence to what for several years was the most difficult job in the Radio. And he put the Hungarian Service back on its feet, behaving properly and broadcasting sensibly and successfully.

But there were two more post-1956 factors that determined the Radio's future course. One was the wise Washington decision, resisting strong pressure, *not* to turn RFE into a news and information radio only. *Comment* continued to play the *defining* role in RFE's broadcasts, as it had always done. It is discussed later in this book (see chapter 5), but its very survival after the trauma of 1956 must obviously be noted in passing.

The second factor was the emergence of a diverse and totally new situation in Eastern Europe itself. Under Stalin there was grey, oppressive uniformity. For three years after his death both the Soviet Union and its satellites were trying to recover from this uniformity and were unsure how to. Then came the explosions of 1956 in Hungary and Poland. After that came Khrushchev's brave decision to opt for reform communism, aimed at securing "communist legitimacy." This meant domestic change for those satellites that might want it. Parameters were still there, of course, but they were widened.

Very soon a patchwork quilt appeared in Eastern Europe. There were movers and nonmovers. Gomułka's Poland lapsed into stagnation. Bulgaria stepped out of its shell and then almost immediately stepped back into it again. But in the other three "RFE countries" things really did move. Hungary quietly began a broad movement of reform. A little later Czechoslovakia began an even broader movement of reform. Romania battened down the hatches at home then surprised everyone by striking out for as much independence as it could get.

This was RFE's new challenge and opportunity. Now it had something in Eastern Europe to respond to and interact with. Now it was called to its historic mission. Now it was necessary more than ever to comment, discern, and appraise. Now it also became an enviable place to work.

2

Recovery in the Sixties

"He who is not against us is with us." János Kádár's incantation in 1961 was a far cry from the hatred of 1956 in Hungary and the vengeful reimposition of Soviet-style socialism in the few years after.

What those words signaled was a new "inclusive" Communist policy in Hungary. It became known as "Kádárism" and lasted over a quarter of a century. Much has been written about Kádár's "New Course," its broadening and deepening. Radio Free Europe's response to it was in two phases. For several years after the revolution most of RFE's Hungarians were too shell-shocked to respond effectively to anything. The revolution itself, its failure, RFE's controversial role, the bad publicity it generated, the divisions within the Hungarian Service itself, the continuing lack of American leadership—they all served to weaken any Radio response to events in Hungary.

But even without these handicaps the evolving Kádárist dynamic would still have put RFE on the back foot. It took real acuity on the part of István Bede and his few allies in the Hungarian Broadcasting Service itself to realize, first, that something seismic was happening and, second, that if RFE was not to lose its audience entirely it must take note of it, respond to it, and keep pressing for more change. RFE needed its own revolution to do this, and it took place in the face of considerable opposition, especially from the large Hungarian diaspora, now reinforced by the sizeable number of refugees from the 1956 Revolution itself. To many in the diaspora, especially strong and vocal now in the United States, any suggestion of a "Kádárist new course" was not just wrong: it could be an indication of communist sympathies on the part of those making it. With some outstanding exceptions, East European exiles in the West, not just Hungarian, tended to be reactionary, nationalistic, and meddling. They made life none the easier for Radio Free Europe.

Some Hungarians in RFE itself refused to accept the authenticity of what was happening in Hungary. "Communists never really change." "Once a Stalinist always a Stalinist!" and so forth. Neither leopards' spots nor tigers' stripes could ever change. The clichés dragged on endlessly. Those mouthing them claimed that they were the voices of realism and of experience as against the fledgling gullibility of the tyro. Nor was such thinking confined to Kádár's Hungary. The Sino-Soviet dispute, it was claimed, was a hoax; so was Romania's semi-independent course and, later, Gorbachev's revolution in the Soviet Union. But however tunnel-visioned, some of these convictions were sincere. Some holding them, though, were not sincere. Their reactions sprang from a "the-worse-the-better" *Anschauung*, seldom confessed but widely held.

Still others were perhaps more profound in their negativism. They later came to believe that Kádárism, through its very success, was eating into the "very soul" of the Hungarian nation. Some intellectuals in both Hungary itself and in exile shared this view. The Hungarian nation, they believed, was being corrupted by the material progress that was admittedly being made. Nationalist intellectuals were convinced that Hungary's historic patrimony, betrayed and lost over sixty years earlier at the Treaty of Trianon after World War I, was being ignored in the new consumerist-internationalist-cosmopolitan rush. They held "Kádárism" responsible.

Disappointment in Poland

Radio Free Europe's Poles never joined the brief *modus vivendi* that came into being between the communist regime and the Catholic Church in Poland in October 1956. But they judiciously and watchfully supported it, and their moderation sealed a covenant between them and the Polish public that lasted till communism was defeated.

RFE's watchfulness was fully justified. Once safe, the new Polish regime shelved the economic and political reforms it had earlier seemed to promise. "Seemed" is the key word here; appearances were deceptive in the Polish October. The October itself was never a confidence trick. Its course saved Poland from Hungary's fate, and the Polish people were fully aware of this. But the situation seemed to have promised them more: comprehensive reforms. So they now forgot the disaster they had averted and became resentful over the future they had been denied. True, there was no regime effort to recollectivize agriculture. Nor was there any serious religious persecution. The secret police, though not disbanded, was reined in. The jamming of Radio Free Europe was officially stopped.[1] Poles felt free, and because they did, they expressed their disappointments more freely.

Most Westerners took some time to realize what was going on. Their relief that Poland had emerged unscathed and their belief that Poland was on a broad track of change led to a continuation of a much too hopeful view of Gomułka. They persisted in thinking him a "liberal" Communist, which he never had been. Gomułka was an ideological "conservative" and an authoritarian by temperament. For several years after 1956 he steadily chipped away at the pedestal Westerners (including Western governments) had built for him. By about 1965 the pedestal had crumbled. So had Gomułka's reputation. He was never a Stalinist, and he did seek to achieve not so much Poland's autonomy as a certain Polish "distinctiveness" in the Soviet bloc. He and Khrushchev maintained mutual respect— they both had a strong interest in doing so—but his relations with Moscow deteriorated after Khrushchev's fall.

More quickly than anyone, Jan Nowak was alive to the erosion of the October reform. It was then that the American State Department made efforts to fence Nowak in and to stop the critical campaign he began to mount (see chapter 3). Basically, what Nowak was now doing was hitching RFE's star to Cardinal Stefan Wyszyński. The Polish Church, though hardly a democratic organization, was the most powerful voice of freedom in Poland. It stoutly maintained that it kept out of politics. No one quite believed that. But Wyszyński, contrary to Western impressions, was far from being a political reactionary. In fact he was a political genius who continually tried to avoid collision with the communist regime. He let Nowak do the colliding.

Czechoslovakia

The Czechoslovak state was called back to life after World War II, but there was still no Czechoslovak nation. Nor did the new state have any more coherence than the old one, established after 1918. In 1948 it fell under communism. But even then, despite the most ruthless centralizing efforts by the communist regime, no coherent state emerged. The Czechoslovak failure became evident in just a few years' time.

The communist regime in Prague immediately set about trying to destroy the two outstanding features of the interwar republic: its democracy and its strong Slovak separatist tendencies. During World War II, Slovak separation had been "fulfilled" by the formation under German patronage of a quasi-independent Slovak state. It was a shameful creation, which had actively connived in the murder of thousands of Slovak Jews by the Nazis in Auschwitz. Still, like the even more hideous Croatian state during World War II, it was a nationalist expression and gave its population a certain confidence and, in their own eyes, a historic vindication.

For different reasons, the war left both Czechs and Slovaks dispirited. RFE's Czechoslovak Service had the chance to rally both. It failed ignominiously because of poor leadership, its refusal to accept Slovak aspirations, and the almost constant criticism and interference from outside.

Indeed for most of the 1950s, Soviet-style socialism seemed to be taking hold in Czechoslovakia. In the meantime Hungary was having its revolution and Poland its October. In Czechoslovakia nothing much seemed to be happening, and RFE made little effort to fill the vacuum. No wonder its Czechoslovak Service was depressed! It was even more depressed when some Western academics began advancing theories about the emergence of a "Czech petty-bourgeois communism," a wedding between Masaryk and Marx, with Lenin officiating.

The Reaction to Khrushchev

Just how wrong such fantasists were was to be shown in the 1960s. But before moving so far, Nikita Khrushchev demands more of our attention. Stalin's death was greeted with relief by Radio Free Europe and by all right-minded human beings. And in the confusion that followed only one thing was now certain: things could not get any worse.

RFE followed closely the power struggle now taking place in the Kremlin, the apparent success of Malenkov, the execution of Beria. Good Kremlinologists, though (and RFE Research already had two), had been following for some time the burrowings of Nikita Khrushchev, and he became Soviet party leader. Though Malenkov as prime minister temporarily got most of the world's attention, experts grew convinced that so long as the communist party remained the center of power in the Soviet Union, its leader would be the most likely new Soviet ruler. This again turned out to be the case, and the world (and RFE) had soon to get used to Nikita Khrushchev, secretary-general of the Communist Party of the Soviet Union, acknowledged (at least for now) as head of the entire communist world and the man to whom much of the third world was turning for support.

The difference with Stalin was the first thing everybody noticed. It could not have been greater. RFE was naturally reassured by this; even its most incorrigible anti-Russians were also reassured that he was the sort of "Ivan" they knew and whose human characteristics they reluctantly conceded. But Khrushchev perplexed them also. He was certainly not the kind of Russian leader history had led them to expect—no gravitas, familiar rather than sinister, a blend of peasant, proletarian, and buffoon. And this led many RFE staff to underrate him. They looked down on his coarseness, habitual mispronunciations, and loud trumpeting of his lowly origins. After every one of his speeches, the Radio corridors and canteen would be buzzing with the "latest" about Khrushchev. Many, too, with better reason, disliked his "bullyboy" characteristics. Yet in RFE, as in the entire world, Khrushchev was recognized as supertheater, another aspect of him calculated to make his predecessor turn over in his grave.

But, clearly, Radio Free Europe judged him mainly by what he did in Eastern Europe. Historically that verdict is mixed. Hesitant hopes were first raised by his "destalinization" speech at the 20ᵗʰ Soviet Party Congress in March 1956, received by RFE from CIA sources and then immediately broadcast.[2] But then hope gave way to tragedy in Hungary in November 1956. And that tragedy made two contradictory things abundantly clear: (1) Eastern Europe's rejection of communism and (2) the Soviet Union's determination to hold Eastern Europe.

Hungary also quickly made Khrushchev an international villain. But slowly and grudgingly opinion about him changed. He began, or stumbled into, a reform program at home. In 1961, he renewed his public campaign against Stalin, dramatically removing the former dictator from his tomb in Red Square alongside the still revered Lenin. But more relevant for RFE was the slow realization that Khrushchev had drastically modified Soviet policy towards Eastern Europe. There were now just two "sacred laws" that the East European regimes had to observe. The first covered domestic policy: reform was acceptable, even encouraged, as long as the communist party ran it. The second covered communist relations: accept Soviet leadership and stay in Comecon and the Warsaw Pact. The imperative now was: get some legitimacy!

This basic shift in Soviet policy inevitably caused a basic change in RFE's policy approach. It had now carefully to stress both the need and the possibility for increased local initiative by the East European regimes themselves. "No excuse now" became the watchword. The once reviled regime of János Kádár now evolved into something of a model. Kádár, too, had become cannily aware that Khrushchev had a special interest in his success. That gave him more freedom.

"Cross-reporting," analyzing, and publicizing "democratizing" developments in one East European country with a view to their being adopted in others became an important duty of RFE Research (see chapter 6) and an important source of programming for the Broadcast Services. The Tito regime in Yugoslavia, since its break for freedom in 1948, was also a valuable "cross-reporting" source. Indeed in the 1960s Hungary and Yugoslavia seemed to be in competition for RFE Research's "cross-reporting championship." And they were soon joined by Czechoslovakia.

It is difficult to exaggerate the shift in RFE policy—philosophy even—that was now coming about. The Radio was moving into the East European communist scene and becoming *involved* in it. Previously, its policy, indeed its *raison d'être*, had been to keep *strictly out*, one of disassociation, even of total rejection. This policy reflected a mentality for which developments like the Prague Spring or Romania's "independence" policy, however different, were equally incomprehensible. They did not conform to the original concepts on which the Radio had been based. The more flexible, historical appraisal of communist rule that now emerged would earlier have been dismissed as idiotic or insidious.

Radio Free Europe's new philosophy emerged almost by stealth in the 1960s. Very few realized it; practically no one talked about it. It governed the Radio's thinking for well over a decade. Then it was scrapped by the new (or old) philosophy under Ronald Reagan.

Jamming's Checkered History

Before proceeding with the sweep of change in Eastern Europe in the sixties and RFE's reaction to it, the jamming of the Radio's broadcasts warrants some attention.

Jamming turned out to be a more complicated issue than many thought. At first all the Services' political programs were jammed, some apparently less effectively than others. Generally, jamming in the capital cities was more systematic than elsewhere, certainly more so than in rural areas. In Prague, for example, jamming could often make listening virtually impossible in the evening, while just a few miles outside the city center, RFE's programs could usually be listened to without much effort.

Jamming was a costly business, too. Permanent jamming everywhere was obviously not considered worthwhile. There were also two types of jamming—local and Soviet. "Local" meant jamming by the country to which the broadcasts were directed. Occasionally, though, the target country would drop its own jamming and use the Soviet service. The Soviet Union had by far the biggest jamming service and could do it more cheaply than its satellites could. Sometimes the local jamming stopped and Soviet jamming would take over, obviously by agreement. This happened mostly in the case of Poland, which, as a political concession, had dropped jamming after the Polish October in 1956. But occasionally the Soviets stepped in, filling the breach as socialist fraternity required.

The motive for starting jamming was obvious, less so for stopping it. In the Polish case and later in the Hungarian, it was not only meant as a political concession to the population but also as proof of regime self-confidence. Only near the bitter end in 1989 did the Czechoslovaks and the Bulgarians stop completely.

The Romanians' case was rather different. They stopped jamming in 1963 just when their "deviation" had become fully known in the West and when there was the distinct possibility that rewards would accrue from it. It was a diplomatic gesture, therefore. But there was another reason, not very encouraging for RFE. Its Romanian Service had for long been ineffective and had steadily lost listeners. Not much to lose, therefore, and probably something solid to gain by stopping jamming. (Later, the Romanian Service became very effective and attracted record audiences).

But making listening impossible or difficult was not the only purpose of jamming. It had a psychological role as well: to make listeners aware that "Big Brother" was everywhere, even in the privacy of the bedroom, where most listening took place. It was thus an instrument of totalitarianism. But even totalitarianism could be stood on its head! Jamming sometimes had a certain rhythm to it and, especially in Romania, some young souls, exuberant in their irreverence, would try to dance to it. "Jiving with the jamming" became something with which even the most ubiquitous totalitarianism could not cope.

Reform and Reaction

Actually the Khrushchev era in Eastern Europe did not end when he fell in 1964. It ended with the Soviet invasion of Czechoslovakia in August 1968. Until then there was change throughout most of the region. Because of this the 1960s were an exciting decade in Radio Free Europe's history. Everyday seemed to bring something new, something hopeful, something that made working at the Radio a stimulus and a challenge.

Poland persisted in being the startling exception. Early in 1968 there was a depressing anti-intellectual campaign led by nationalist-Stalinists, with strong anti-Semitic undertones. And right at the end of 1970 came the rising, mainly on the Baltic coast, against the imposition of steep food price rises that led to the fall of Gomułka.

Before that, there was still further retrogression from the hopes and illusions of October 1956. For a few years Poland became almost dull! A regime campaign against the Roman Catholic Church began early in the decade and reached its climax in the middle of it. Every effort was made to show how reactionary Cardinal Wyszyński was in the context of the sweeping church reforms set in motion by Pope John XXIII. RFE's Polish Broadcasting Service rallied to the cardinal's defense. The result was still closer confidence and contact between RFE and the Polish Church, with Rome a frequent meeting place between dignitaries of both organizations.

Jan Nowak was surely never dull. Every day was a new day for him, harassing (but also energizing) his bosses in the Front Office, his colleagues in News and in Research, and his subordinates in Polish Broadcasting. He traveled the length and breadth of Western Europe to meet visitors from Poland—regime and anti-regime officials, intellectuals, clerical and lay. And whilst Nowak was dynamic, Gomułka, his principal adversary, was painfully in decline, now with little to show except a choleric temper. Analyzing every speech made by him, RFE's research analysts soon realized this deterioration.

But if Poland was not moving, its neighbors were. Khrushchev's dismissal in 1964 was widely expected to see a reversion to the *status quo ante*. But Hungary kept on moving. Kádár knew that the Kremlin's new leaders did not like his reform, but he also surmised that they were anxious to signal no big change in Eastern Europe. Moscow was, in any case, fully confronted with communism's greatest ever schism, the Sino-Soviet dispute. It wanted calm among its satellites.

Economic reform, though modified, continued in Hungary, as did beneficial commercial contacts with the West. The population benefited from the steady, perceptible rise in living standards. This was important for Radio Free Europe, too. The Hungarian Service's economic coverage was second only to that of the Polish Service in quality. After understandable caution in greeting the new changes, the Hungarian Service had vigorously shown its approval. It was gratified by the support that many eminent economists in Hungary itself were giving to the reform and took steps to carry and explain their writings to its listeners. Criticism there certainly was, but, almost without exception, it was qualified and constructive. Kádár was helping to bring Radio Free Europe to maturity!

Kádár's lifting of restrictions on Western travel for Hungarians became a "flagship" feature of his policy in the 1960s. Again Radio Free Europe welcomed it, urging others to do likewise. Members of the Hungarian emigration also welcomed it, once they had got over their incredulity. Some of them, though, soon found that a month-long invasion by up to five of their "long lost" family could be a mixed blessing. A very costly one, too! So much so that some émigrés began to speak ruefully of "Kádár's revenge."

RFE Rocks

But it was not so much Kádár as an RFE innovation that really set Hungary alight. This was the introduction as early as 1958 by the Hungarian Service of "rock" music programs. They were so immediately popular that their broadcast time was lengthened and their scope extended. An important cultural link was thus established. Some of the older generation Hungarians at RFE were aghast when such "trivia" began, but they soon began rocking round the clock when audience response became known. RFE's Hungarian listeners increased rapidly, and some of its youthful listeners began to partake also of its more serious fare—news, for example, and even the occasional political program.

Thus, Radio Free Europe's Hungarian Service, in the doldrums since the revolution, began to win back its audience. The new music programs undoubtedly helped, a reflection of an important new fact: RFE was "with it." Nor did the Hungarian Service's success go unnoticed within RFE itself. The other four services became "rockers" too! After gulping hard, even Jan Nowak rocked. Throughout Eastern Europe the old standard communist fare—peasant folk tunes and rousing red marches—began to sound impermissibly "square."

The star of the RFE's new music programs was the Hungarian, Géza Ekecs ("László Cseke" on air). Even before he began his music adventure, Ekecs had become a first-class general broadcaster. A "natural" if ever there was one, he became a true RFE immortal. But his music program also made him a Magyar celebrity. After liberation, on visiting Hungary he was welcomed as a folk hero. No one deserved it more.

Although István Bede began the salutary changes on the Hungarian Service, it was his successor, József (Joe) Szabados, who became their true spirit. Educated in France and Belgium, Szabados had worked for several years in Radio Free Europe's office in New York. He was a younger man with a Romanian wife, an international outlook, and a strong admiration for the United States. He was very much at home with younger people both from the West and from Hungary. Under Szabados it was often not a question of RFE responding to opinion in Hungary but of opinion in Hungary responding to RFE. Some older Hungarian listeners did not know what had hit them. And many members of the diaspora grew increasingly disaffected. Eventually they backed George Urban in getting rid of Szabados in 1986. He died in 2004, another of Radio Free Europe's heroes.

Czechoslovakia's Glory Years

The developments in Hungary undoubtedly played some role in stirring Czechoslovakia from its slumbers. But its arousal, though slow in coming, soon gathered speed. When the sixties began, party leader Antonin Novotný seemed firmly in control. In 1960 Czechoslovakia was officially claimed to have evolved from a "People's" Republic to a "Socialist" Republic, the first satellite to do so, obviously a sign of Soviet approval of its stability through the fifties. Two years later Novotný seemed to manage the 12th Party Congress in fine political style.

But all was not well behind this confident posturing. Minister of the Interior Rudolf Barak, second only to Novotný in the hierarchy, was suddenly purged in 1961. Unlike Novotný, Barak had the common touch and, strange for an interior minister, was relatively popular. But he was overambitious, and this led to his downfall. Novotný was still strong enough to defeat him. Barak was progressively stripped of all his posts, arrested, tried, and sentenced to fifteen years in jail. He had tried to turn the situation to his advantage but had seriously misjudged it. Destalinization, the reforms in Hungary, the changes of party leadership in Poland, Hungary, Bulgaria, and the Soviet Union itself throughout the fifties—everything seemed to be conspiring in Barak's favor, except his enemy Novotný.

RFE's response to Barak was understandably cautious, equivocal even. It could not see how a communist interior minister could be the convinced reformer that Barak purported to be. Still, anybody was better than Novotný! Hence the equivocation. It seemed, though, that this caution was justified. Subsequent conversations in Prague with Czechs about Barak only strengthened the doubts about him.

But Novotný's turn was coming. His eventual downfall removed the last brick that had kept Czech Stalinism standing. There were two main catalysts of change: one was an economic situation that seemed headed for catastrophe; the other was the reemergence of Slovak nationalism. True, Novotný astonishingly clung to power for another seven years, till the beginning of 1968. But in those seven years he lost more than his power: he lost his relevance. A slow-fuse revolution engulfed both him and Czechoslovakia.

The Czechoslovak economy escaped World War II relatively unharmed: it was when the communists seized power in 1948 that the rot set in. But the economy had been so basically strong that it took about fifteen years for it to face collapse. There had been ample signs of impending doom, but the lightning really struck in 1963 when several key economic indicators were lower than in the previous year and the standard of living slipped. Novotný had no way of either explaining or rectifying this. His only concern was to save himself.

Such economic disaster—and it was occurring throughout most of Eastern Europe—was bound to generate ideas and calls for reform. The most notable early call came from the Soviet Union. It was 1962; Khrushchev was still in power, a leader who encouraged ideas, both sensible and silly. Professor Y. G. Liberman's article "The Plan, Profits and Premiums" was carried in the Soviet party daily *Pravda*, not just hidden away in any specialist journal. The essence of Liberman's argument was that profit should be regarded as the motor of economic activity. He described the existing socialist system as one of waste, rigidity, and incongruities. Thus the genie was out of the bottle. Some of Liberman's arguments sounded like the principles of the Polish NEM (New Economic Model) of 1956. The important thing, though, was that it inspired a spate of similar, but more exciting, articles in the Soviet satellites.

Czechoslovakia led the way. Everybody knew that there had always been talent there. Debates on economic change opened up, mainly in the economic press. The most significant reform contributions came from Professor Ota Šik, very much a pillar of the Communist establishment. Šik knew that influential elements in the party now realized that changes had to be made. Subsequently he and others realized that only the most radical solutions would do. Nor were they simply confining their ideas to the economy. "Even under socialism the individual is more important than the state," wrote one courageous reformer. Heresies like this began to appear in print, not in dissident leaflets but in communist newspapers.

In both the Czech lands and Slovakia the do-nothing days were over. But in Slovakia the calls for reform became inextricably linked with nationalism—Slovak nationalism, not Czechoslovak nationalism. Slovak nationalism was as much against Prague as against Moscow. In the Czech lands it was not nationalism but democracy that pushed to the fore.

The secret police throughout the country, whose powers of intimidation had once been awesome, now began to feel intimidated themselves. Freedom of speech, unknown since 1948, returned at first tentatively, then in a flood. So did press confidence. New tribunes of the media began to appear in both Prague and Bratislava; as journalists felt fewer constraints, they became progressively bolder. Media "stars" shone brightly every morning in print and every night over the airwaves.

It is impossible to describe the excitement in Radio Free Europe as these events were unfolding. Many people, not just Czechs and Slovaks, began showing up at work at barbarously early hours to be first with the news from Czechoslovakia. At first the Czechs could not believe their eyes and ears but then responded with full supportive sincerity. The real intellectual talent that had always been there among RFE's Czechs now came to full flower. Among the other Broadcast Services the Hungarians responded well to the Czech events; it was good to have a neighbor in the reform business! But traditional East European prejudices began to show too. The Poles, to no one's surprise, were the least gracious about Czechoslovakia. They reported fully what was going on, but their few commentaries were more perfunctory than enthusiastic. They regarded Poles as being the real standard bearers of freedom. To see the Czechs, of all people, setting the pace, especially when Poland itself was relatively quiet, was a humiliation too much to bear!

The other two Broadcast Services, the Romanian and the Bulgarian, with much less broadcasting time than the larger services, also responded well to the "Prague Spring," as it was now becoming known. Besides, both countries also showed some signs of reform. In Romania Nicolae Ceauşescu, who became party leader in 1965, seemed set on some relaxation. Even Bulgaria seemed to be nodding its approval.

When, how, would it all end? That question crossed the mind of every Radio Free Europe employee, not least that of Radio Free Europe's then director, Ralph Walter. Walter had been a member of Griffith's policy staff during the Hungarian Revolution in 1956. He was only too aware, therefore, of what could go wrong. The Czechoslovak Service, too, thrilled though most of its members were, never lost its judgment. Its broadcasts began to urge caution as soon events in Prague looked as if they might be spiraling out of control. This was measured broadcasting, nothing like the chaos that had prevailed over Hungary in 1956.

When Novotný was finally ousted early in 1968, the path was open for even more daring reform. A Slovak, Alexander Dubček, succeeded Novotný. The little that was known about him was favorable—a moderate Slovak nationalist who still believed in Czechoslovakia, and a moderate supporter of reform. He seemed to be reassuring to everybody, including Moscow. But Dubček's tragedy was that he was so weak he soon reassured nobody. Still, in early 1968 he seemed an inspired choice. The Soviets probably thought that their "twin imperatives" of communist party leadership and Soviet alliance would be preserved.

The "doves" in the Moscow leadership were apparently ready

to give the new Dubček leadership time to settle and to conform. But the "hawks" were already impatient, convinced that Dubček was too weak to stem the tide of "bourgeois democracy" and that Czechoslovakia was already slipping out of Moscow's control. The "hawks" were proved right. By the spring of 1968 the march to democracy in Czechoslovakia was unstoppable, except by Soviet tanks. But in the West, even as the "Spring" became summer, many experts still thought that these two Soviet imperatives could be preserved (I did too). Therefore, the Soviets had no "excuse" for invading Czechoslovakia.

Obviously the Soviets had no "excuse" at all, whatever the circumstances. But they read the situation right. The point about Eastern Europe, including the Baltic republics in the Soviet Union, was that unhindered reform anywhere, Bulgaria and Romania included, was bound to lead toward a Western-type democracy. Flawed to be sure, very flawed in some countries, but recognizable. After twenty years of "real existing socialism," the only possible alternative (and many communists were believing this too) was Western-oriented democracy. Not necessarily with American-type capitalism thrown in, but the *political* democracy that both North America and Western Europe shared. And once the momentum towards political and economic change had developed, as it had in Czechoslovakia, then to imagine that it would or could stop or reverse was to lose touch with reality.

There was no need for any inquest at RFE after the Soviet invasion of August 20, 1968, as there had been over Hungary in 1956, no need to examine Czechoslovak programming in those fateful hours and days. And Ralph Walter must take much credit for the Radio's responsibility. He exercised a strict "hands on" supervision over the Czechoslovak broadcasts during and immediately after the Soviet-led invasion. The broadcast autonomy that all the departments normally enjoyed at the Radio had been lessened considerably as the crisis began to mount.

But much credit must also go to the Czechoslovak Service itself; its leadership and entire staff responded to events with skill and moderation. They cooperated fully with Walter and his staff. Some of them had lived through Hungary in 1956; they knew the stakes and the dangers involved. Especially in the first few days after August 20, some of the Czechoslovak programs, in terms of sympathy, sobriety, and quality, were among the best that Radio Free Europe ever broadcast. RFE's Czechoslovaks came out of their ordeal with great credit. They had responded nobly to a historic challenge. It was *their* finest hour too.

Exploiting the Sino-Soviet Dispute

While the Prague Spring had been flowering, so had the Sino-Soviet dispute. Each was different, but each showed the basic weakness of communism as both an ideology and a system. It took some experts in the West a long time to accept that there was a Sino-Soviet dispute at all. "They're looking at everything in nineteenth-century terms," said one American professor, dismissing colleagues naïve enough to chase hares like this. Then there were those exiles, some early on at Radio Free Europe, who were sure the whole thing was a hoax, the sort of thing that fooled innocent Americans. Some former communists, too, suckled on conspiracy, were sure that this was so.

RFE's American management was quickly on to the Sino-Soviet dispute. It urged the five Broadcast Services to carry contrasting and conflicting Soviet and Chinese press articles. It even got special money from Washington to get these articles translated and to have them broadcast past midnight after the end of the normal hours of broadcasting. Not all the Broadcast Services responded enthusiastically to this new opportunity. The Poles were quite perfunctory about it. What had the Sino-Soviet dispute got to do with them? But they came round when several intellectuals in Poland expressed interest. RFE got considerable credit for its initiative. One U.S. senator told us we were "on top of things," "clocked," in fact.

Discovering Albania

Radio Free Europe had, at its inception, nearly started broadcasting to Albania, but didn't.[3] Apart from those who had read Edith Durham there was little interest.

There was not much eagerness therefore, to follow the Albanian minirift with Moscow, which first became obvious at the end of the 1950s. But though its existence could not be denied, its importance was. The famous German commentator, Richard Löwenthal, on a visit to Radio Free Europe in 1960, described Enver Hoxha as a "little twerp." But RFE's management, already aware of the Sino-Soviet dispute, was also soon aware of the implications of a "Chinese bridgehead" in Europe. Louis Zanga, an Albanian-American researcher, was hired from Washington to put Albanian analysis at the Radio on a professional footing. The Broadcast Services used his papers in programming, as did Western scholars and journalists. Radio Free Europe saw Enver Hoxha as more than a "little twerp."

I was the man Louis Zanga replaced as Albanian analyst. I must say I enjoyed my makeshift stint, especially the numerous requests for help and information I got from interested Westerners who evidently knew even less about Albania than I did. Knowing not a word of Albanian, I was dependent on the English translations of Enver Hoxha's speeches and of key newspaper articles carried by the official Albanian Telegraphic Agency (ATA). Hoxha's speeches were well put together, breathing fire against "Soviet revisionists" and Nikita Khrushchev personally. Hoxha often drove his primed audiences into paroxysms of outrage. ATA, with a nice dramatic touch, would describe their uproar as "animation in the hall!" Indeed, "animation in the hall" became a favorite term in RFE's Research Department. Its members often used it when referring to the wrathful outbursts of some of our superiors.

Romania's Diplomatic Skills

If there was one thing the Romanian communist leadership seemed to share with the nation it governed, it was a certain prudence. Yet in the late 1950s it entered a game bound to be dangerous no matter how prudently played.

Nikita Khrushchev, as said earlier, was a man responsive to ideas. Some were big ideas too. Stalin established Comecon (or CEMA), the Council for Mutual Economic Assistance, in 1949. Having founded it, Stalin then mostly forgot about it, and each Soviet satellite proceeded to industrialize comprehensively on Soviet lines. Romania set about building its huge "flagship" iron and steel complex at Galați on the Danube delta. Several similar, if smaller, complexes were built, or begun, throughout Romania, a country rich in natural resources. Indeed, heavy industry generally became synonymous with Soviet-style socialism.

It was typical of Khrushchev that, having first approved of Romania's orthodox heavy industrial program, he very soon came to have doubts about it. He was now persuaded that the satellites should concentrate on the economic activity that nature had made most suitable for them. This was the essence of his new panacea, "the international socialist division of labor." It meant trouble for socialist Romania. Looking back now, in the retrospect of well over forty years, it would have been a good strategy for all the East European satellites to have adopted Khrushchev's ideas. But for the Romanian regime, just over ten years in power, groping for legitimation in a complex country, originally weak and still weak, it would have meant a crippling loss of whatever prestige it had and whatever legitimacy it aspired to.

What were its options then? Capitulation to Khrushchev was the obvious one, but the Romanian leader, Gheorghe Gheorghiu-Dej, canny enough to have survived so far, knew that capitulation would probably mean his own political oblivion. Besides, the bloc situation was propitious for resisting, and it was now that Gheorghiu-Dej read Moscow's embarrassment brilliantly. The Sino-Soviet schism was well under way, and he knew that this enabled Bucharest to take advantage of the restrictions it placed on Moscow's freedom of action. There was also a distinct thaw developing in East-West relations that was giving more opportunities to Bucharest. Finally there was no danger whatever of Gheorghiu-Dej flouting, or forgetting, the Soviet Union's "two imperatives" for all the East European satellites. Party control was stricter in Romania than anywhere in Eastern Europe except Albania. As for bloc loyalty, Gheorghiu-Dej, and later Ceauşescu, did often seem to severely test Soviet tolerance. But the Romanian communists had clearly inherited some of the diplomatic ability their predecessors had shown. Throughout the twentieth century, Romanian diplomats had negotiated with skill and nerve, and were blessed with luck.

The progress of the Romanian "deviation," as it often came to be called, is well enough known. The last great step in its progress before Gheorghiu-Dej died in 1965 was the declaration of the

Romanian party's Central Committee in April 1964, often called "Romania's Declaration of Independence." It was a bold assertion of the freedom of every party within the world communist movement and a rejection of all forms of tutelage inside it. It also defended, indirectly, several points the Chinese were making against Moscow.

But still, the Romanians were obviously anxious to avoid a total split between the Chinese and the Soviets and were urging both sides to resume negotiations. In March 1964 a Romanian delegation led by Prime Minister Ion Gheorghe Maurer went to Beijing to plead with the Chinese to talk to the Soviets. Maurer was the best diplomat the communist world ever produced. In the whole twentieth century there was probably none better in the entire free world either. His, essentially, was old school diplomacy, with similarities to Romania's diplomacy in the Balkan Wars before World War I and later in Paris during the World War I settlements. Woodrow Wilson once said during these negotiations that the delegates from the Balkan nations did not "represent their facts in the same way (as others), and there would always be something not quite clear." The technique still seemed to work! The Romanians probably knew also that Khrushchev's position in the Kremlin was weakening and that this made any punitive Soviet action against them highly unlikely, at least for the present.

They were right about Khrushchev. He was deposed in October 1964. But the Romanians knew that Gheorghiu-Dej, their own leader, was also nearing death with cancer. He died in June 1965, and Nicolae Ceaușescu replaced him. In fairly quick succession, Ceaușescu soon became an internationally admired figure, then an internationally despised and domestically hated one.

But Ceaușescu early made it clear that there would be no let-up in Romania's "independence" course. He established relations with West Germany when Moscow was virtually ordering all its East European allies not to. But much more excitement, and tension, was to come. Ceaușescu opposed the Soviet-led invasion of Czechoslovakia in August 1968. He did so openly, too, criticizing the Soviet move in the clearest terms. The world waited nervously. President Johnson urged the Soviets not to "unleash the dogs of war." There were obviously "hawks" in the Kremlin on this issue, too. But they did not prevail; Romania was spared. Ceaușescu continued his nationalist policy and this meant clashing with Moscow on a number of issues throughout the seventies, the most important of which was a Soviet demand for a channel through Romanian territory to enable their troops to get most easily to Bulgaria. The Romanians resisted, and the Soviets apparently dropped the idea.

The "Romanian deviation" brought RFE's Romanian service into the limelight. In the first few years of its existence it had been, along with the Bulgarians, the Radio's poor relations, with between seven and eight hours per day of broadcast time (the rest had about seventeen) and nothing much really to broadcast about. Now Romania was on the pages, sometimes the front pages, of every world newspaper of repute. Romania had arrived. And so had the Romanian Service of Radio Free Europe.

How did RFE's Romanians react to their country's fame? At first, with bemusement or plain disbelief. Many continued to dismiss the reports in the press as groundless speculation. What some betrayed was a psychological determination not to believe them. It was an article of faith with most Romanian exiles that Romania's communists had always been a tiny clique of fanatics or opportunists. Also, most were not real "Romanians," by which was meant they were mainly Jews with a few Hungarians, the odd Bulgarian, and not a few Gypsies thrown in, all put in power and kept there by the Soviets. It was simply impossible to believe that they could either defy the Soviet Union or invoke any patriotic feeling amongst the "real Romanians." "Rumors to the contrary," were, again, the products of Western naïveté, journalistic prostitution, or yet another hoax.

It was certainly no hoax. The valid evidence mounted and soon became almost universally accepted. It was, in fact, RFE's Romanian audience that needed most convincing. But there remained two or three Romanians at RFE who lost their analytical moorings over the "Romanian deviation" and never fully recovered them.

The director of the Romanian Service when it all began was Ghita Ionescu. He had responded to it with some speed and ability but was later unfairly dismissed after some squalid intrigue. He took himself off to England and a distinguished academic career at Manchester University. Noel Bernard replaced him. Bernard had earlier been Romanian Service Director, also dismissed unfairly, this time through exile intrigue, largely because he was Jewish and not a "real Romanian." His ego was as boundless as his energy. He was RFE's most brilliant broadcast journalist ever. Under him, the Romanian Broadcast Service rapidly increased its audience, with Bernard himself becoming a household name in Romania. There was a story doing the rounds in Romania in the middle seventies that revealed this:

Ceauşescu, visiting an obscure part of Romania, knocks on the door of a broken-down farmhouse. An aged peasant opens the door and the conversation goes as follows:

Peasant: "Who the hell are you"?
Ceauşescu: "Don't you know me"?
Peasant: "No"
Ceauşescu: "Don't you watch television"?
Peasant: "Don't have a television"
Ceauşescu: "What about newspapers"?
Peasant:"Can't read."
Ceauşescu: (tetchily) "You must have a radio then"
Peasant: "Yeah, we have a radio"
Ceauşescu: "Well, I'm very often on the radio. Don't you know me now"?

The peasant's eyes open wide. He trundles off, shouting to his wife, "Lenuto, Lenuto, come quick, it's Noel Bernard."

RFE's Romanian Service had arrived.

3

Tensions in the West

Radio Free Europe was a thorn in the side of the European communist governments. But it was a thorn in the side of the American democratic government, too. As East-West state relations improved, flowering later into détente, the State Department began receiving a growing number of complaints, especially from Warsaw, about RFE broadcasts. And the more attention the State Department gave these complaints, the more they grew.

The Radio's difficulties with the State Department stemmed from the crucial difference between their basic tasks. RFE's main obligation was towards the *societies* of Eastern Europe. The State Department's was to conduct relations with the *states* of Eastern Europe. This is not to say that the State Department did not care for East European societies. Institutionally it did and its diplomats did too, collectively and singly. And, in general, the government of the United States has shown a greater concern for human welfare than any other government. But the priorities and the emphases of State and RFE obviously differed, and it was in the difference that the difficulties between the two lay.

RFE was always basically hostile toward the East European communist governments, because even the most reformist of them still denied their societies the essential rights they increasingly craved—the "democratic deficit" always. The State Department recognized this deficit and worked quietly to have it reduced. But at the same time it had to develop relations of many kinds with the communist governments. It found RFE's "single-mindedness" irksome. For RFE the cup was always half-empty; for State it could often be half-full. And RFE always felt that State, representing the awesome power of the United States, could get what it wanted from the East European states without seeming to encourage their nagging campaign against RFE.

The CIA-State Muddle

After the Hungarian Revolution the State Department assumed a "macromanagement," or "macrosupervision," of Radio Free Europe's broadcast policy. The CIA link, though, continued in financing, management, and "routine" broadcasting. Some CIA officials continued to be posted to RFE in Munich, often filling positions on the roster for which they were barely qualified. Cross-links continued between the Radio's leadership in Munich and CIA's headquarters in Langley, Virginia. Links were also maintained between the Radio in Munich and the CIA representative attached to the large American Consulate General in Munich, as they were with CIA officials attached to the main U.S. army base in Munich. It was almost as if nothing had changed. But it was a messy arrangement, a "triangulation," destined to go wrong. What, for example, was the difference between "macromanagement" and "micromanagement"? Where did CIA policy management leave off and State Department management begin? As it was, Eastern Europe was remarkably quiet in the years following the Hungarian Revolution and the Polish October. Therefore, the new arrangement was largely untested.

Would it have been better had a completely new arrangement been made after 1956, with RFE being taken from the CIA and placed under a new quasigovernmental organization, as it was years later in the early seventies? (See chapter 4.) Most Washingtonians tend to argue that if a clean break had been attempted "too early" after the Hungarian Revolution, RFE would almost certainly not have survived. And too extensive a reorganization would have been seen as a major American defeat in the Cold War. Even an amalgamation with the Voice of America would have been seen, rightly, as the elimination of RFE.

There was also an important family factor to be taken into consideration. John Foster Dulles was secretary of state in the Eisenhower administration; Allen Dulles, his brother, was director of the CIA. This fact may have helped save RFE from elimination in 1956, but it may also have led to the messy "compromise" after 1956. But whereas the CIA was spared loss of its Radio and the accompanying public comment, there must have been considerable frustration in the State Department over the decision that was eventually taken. State was left with a vague power of supervision of RFE's broadcast policy content. The "rest" remained with the CIA. Indeed, some of the State Department's persisting censoriousness regarding the Radio's programs should probably be seen in the light of its limited, ill-defined new powers and to its "turf war" with the CIA on the subject of RFE. Put that "turf war" factor along with the preoccupation with mending state relations and with the quirky egos of some American diplomats on the Eastern Europe circuit, then there seems to be ample explanation for the State Department's permanent suspicion of RFE.

It consistently made trouble for the Radio over Poland in the late 1950s. Władysław Gomułka's return to power in Poland in October 1956 had prevented the Polish October from becoming the Polish Revolution (see chapter 1). The State Department had every reason to have respected him. And though it seldom admitted it, State must also have been grateful to RFE for its performance during the Polish October. Afterwards, though, State began to see Nowak as Polish Problem Number One.

But that was precisely when Nowak turned out to be more politically sagacious than the State Department. State thought Gomułka would turn out to be another Tito. Nowak knew he was an orthodox Communist and would soon show it. State thought he would go forward, Nowak knew he would drift back. One State Department official I spoke to as late as 1965 worked himself into a quite undiplomatic lather about Nowak. To most American diplomats he was not so much a loose cannon as a loose howitzer. The embassy in Warsaw soon challenged him, and in the summer of 1959 Ambassador Jacob Beam asked in effect for RFE's Polish broadcasts to be stopped. Indeed, Beam was certainly the spearhead of a concerted State Department move against RFE. The whole future of RFE became the subject of debate. But the storm passed, thanks in part to the strong support for RFE of Vice President Richard Nixon, whose recent visit to Warsaw had been made a great success thanks mainly to RFE's coverage of it.

Two salient points emerged from the "Beam Crisis" of 1959: (1) It showed that the State Department was determined now to exercise its right to supervise RFE's broadcasts; and (2) the influence of RFE in Poland was openly admitted to be central. Some State Department officials as well as some Polish communist reformers in Warsaw later even began blaming RFE for Gomułka's drift towards orthodoxy.

Two personal points also emerged from the crisis. (1) Nowak was strengthened but he also realized that neither he, nor the Polish Service, nor RFE as a whole could survive another crisis like the Beam crisis. The result was that, though the Polish Service programs did not essentially change in character, their tone was modified. In any case, Nowak's situation was made all the easier as Gomułka's rule got worse. And, (2) Jacob Beam, who later became ambassador to Czechoslovakia and then the Soviet Union, eventually changed his attitude decisively. He became reconciled to RFE and in the 1970s actually became chairman of the Radio's Board of Directors in Washington. I met him frequently in that capacity. He was obviously a real gentleman, but I never knew him well enough to ask why he took the road to Damascus.

So Gomułka continued his misrule and RFE continued criticizing him. He proceeded to alienate Wyszyński and the Catholic Church thoroughly. During the Prague Spring in 1968 he sided with the East German leader, Walter Ulbricht, in persistently demanding that the Soviet Union halt the Czech reform by any means possible. He also allowed the Polish Communist Party to indulge in a nasty bout of anti-Semitism in early 1968.

But his most chronic failings were in the economy. For these he was constantly taken to task by Michael Gamarnikow, the Polish Service's senior economics editor. Gomułka once even thought fit to attack Gamarnikow by name at a party Central Committee meeting. And it was economics that finally brought Gomułka down. In December 1970, immediately after a great Polish diplomatic victory through West German recognition of the Oder-Neisse Line, he announced sharp price increases on a series of basic foodstuffs. He obviously hoped the Poles would swallow the increase out of gratitude. They didn't. A number of strikes broke out on the Baltic coast and Polish troops killed at least fifty strikers. Gomułka had to go.

The Polish Service's coverage of the December 1970 strikes was as statesmanlike as it had been during the Polish October in 1956. It welcomed the accession of Edward Gierek to the party leadership. It also welcomed the winning ways of Gierek's early rule. But then history repeated itself. The State Department began another love affair, this time with Gierek. And as Radio Free Europe's early welcome for Gierek changed into increasingly critical appraisals of his economic policy, so the State Department's pressure on the Radio resumed. One junior Warsaw embassy man admiringly described Gierek to me as "a man of steel" and rejected any criticism of him. It was the post–Polish October phase yet again. In its defense, it must be said that the State Department's enthusiasm for Gierek was generally shared by West European governments and by many journalists and academics. Once again it was Michael Gamarnikow who stood out with his trenchant criticisms. The American ambassador in Warsaw threw a fit, and Polish official complaints about RFE were approvingly passed on to Washington.

But Gamarnikow's analysis was unassailable; and within six years, in 1976, Gierek imposed his own fatal set of price rises. His incompetence had finally caught up with him. There were strikes in most of the country and clear evidence of widespread police brutality. Most important, the 1956 alliance between workers and intellectuals was now restored. The price increases, as in 1971, had to be withdrawn, and Gierek, though he clung to power for nearly four more years, now found his credibility shattered. RFE was again vindicated. The general feeling began to sink into the State Department that RFE might know more about Poland than it did.

Heat on the Romanian Service

The Polish people's repudiation of Gierek in 1976 and the rapid unraveling of communist rule in Poland thereafter resulted in a lessening of State Department pressure on the Polish Service. But the pressure now shifted to the Romanian Service.

Virtually everyone in the West admired the "Romanian deviation." RFE admired it, too. But the admiration for Romanian audacity and the awareness of its impact on the Cold War led many to excuse or deliberately overlook the rapid deterioration of the domestic situation in Romania. The first few years of Ceauşescu's rule were "promising" in domestic policy as well as in foreign and bloc policy. Unquestionably these were years of hope inside Romania. The standard of living improved; the security apparatus appeared curbed; greater freedom of speech was allowed; cultural restrictions were relaxed. There was some optimism in both Romania and in the West. Dick Burks, then policy director at RFE, said publicly in 1966 that "in a few years" there would be "as much cultural freedom in Romania as there was in Switzerland." An American embassy official in Bucharest, stopping over in Munich on his way to Washington in early 1968, told me that Ceauşescu's leading team had "resemblances to John Kennedy's Camelot."

Neither my colleagues in Research nor I were prepared to go that far, but we were also optimistic in general about Romania's domestic prospects. The big fear, heightened immeasurably after Ceauşescu's defiance of Moscow over the invasion of Czechoslovakia in August 1968, was of a possible Soviet move now against Romania. This nervousness only served to invest Ceauşescu with well-nigh heroic qualities. He made several visits to West European countries and the United States and was given the kind of royal welcomes he so obviously liked. He and his wife, Elena, were given free room and board at Buckingham Palace, and Elena was even awarded an honorary doctorate by Birmingham University in England.

Deterioration in Romania

Ceauşescu's nationalism certainly seemed to be dangerous at times. But in domestic policy the early hopes were dashed, and Romania was plunged into a pit of fear, tyranny, inefficiency, poverty, nepotism, and misgovernment. True, Ceauşescu lacked the murderousness of a Stalin, but his regime (always excepting Enver Hoxha's in Albania) came closer to Stalinism than any other European communist regime since 1953. It has been plausibly argued that it was Ceauşescu's visits to China and especially North

Korea in 1971 that made him a political madman. But to explain why Chairmen Kim and Mao had so drastic an effect on him is a matter more for psychologists than students of politics.

As Ceauşescu's tyranny worsened, the Romanian Service at RFE sharpened its criticisms of him. Noel Bernard led the attacks, and occasionally they did exceed the required bounds of moderation. For this he had to be called to order by his supervisors inside the Radio. But the State Department's criticisms became an onslaught. Washington, as it had over Gomułka and Gierek in Poland, showed a painful, deliberate slowness in realizing what was going on in Romania. It simply could not, or would not, admit the speed and extent of Ceauşescu's departure from even the most remotely acceptable norms of governance. It was only towards the end of the 1970s that the State Department quietly accepted that it had been indeed as wrong about Romania as it had been about Poland.

Explaining State

How can such unawareness this time be explained? Obviously, the convictions of many exiles that the American diplomatic corps, along with the Western press corps, was riddled with communists or fellow travelers can be dismissed as primitive nonsense. More plausibly, it was sometimes put down to "localitis." Roughly speaking, localitis is the process whereby a diplomat becomes so enamored or bewitched by the country in which he or she is serving that his or her judgment becomes unprofessionally skewed in favor of its government.

It is easy to see how localitis can be alluring. But it could become a problem, too, especially in communist countries. Again, one is forced to return to the distinction, and often to the collision, between state relations and social relations, that is, to the distinction that justified the existence of Radio Free Europe. Did localitis really refer to a genuine sympathy for the history, culture, and character of the host country? If it did, then presumably there should also have been some understanding for an institution like RFE, which after all was bent on defending most aspects of the national heritages that the ruling communist regimes were out to undermine.

Was American diplomacy really shifting during the 1960s, and especially the 1970s, towards the traditional European diplomatic emphasis on state relations even where communist countries were concerned? (See discussion at the start of this chapter.) Was the State Department now ready to excuse or ignore growing misgovernment in a communist state for the sake of an undoubted Cold War advantage over the Soviet Union?

In other words was a greater "realism" overtaking American foreign policy, and was Ceauşescu's Romania the first obvious example of it? It certainly looked like it. "Greater realism" was evident in American policy toward Ceauşescu right from 1965 and was made abundantly clear under Henry Kissinger's "Westphalian" doctrines, pursued under President Nixon. Most dramatically of all, this policy was evident in the case of China, and the Romanian case was a much smaller offshoot of that. Nixon's state visit to Bucharest as early as 1969 was a similar case in point. Although Nixon subsequently claimed that the idea was entirely his own, it was indeed all very Kissingerian! Kissinger was indeed known to be ready to close down RFE (and RL) if a "Great Arrangement" could be made with the Soviet Union. It was left to Zbigniew Brzezinski under Jimmy Carter to stem the Westphalian tide.

The View from Bonn

The small town of Bonn, Germany, often loomed large on Radio Free Europe's radar. Détente was ushered in about fifteen years after the Federal Republic of Germany achieved sovereign status. But West Germany was never totally sovereign. It was American protected, therefore basically American controlled. And as long as the Cold War continued, the Germans reluctantly accepted this status.

But the 1970s saw the Social Democrats (SPD) in power in Bonn, first under Willy Brandt and then under Helmut Schmidt. The SPD government was at the forefront of détente, recognizing East Germany (the German Democratic Republic, or GDR), establishing diplomatic relations with the other East European communist regimes, increasing economic, commercial, and cultural relations with them, and generally seeking to undo the enormous harm that Hitler's Germany had done to the German image. Just as Konrad Adenauer had (successfully) concentrated on restoring

German respectability in Western Europe and North America, so Willy Brandt took on the same mission in Eastern Europe and the Soviet Union. This was the *Ostpolitik*. It would be too much to say that Brandt completely succeeded, but he *began* the process, and the warmth of his personality and his humanity made a deep impression throughout the world.

But, to paraphrase an old Jewish question, was he good or bad for Radio Free Europe? In truth, Willy Brandt, a former mayor of West Berlin, genuinely stood for the principle of free speech, a right he knew was denied to the people of Eastern Europe. But he was worried about RFE and would have liked to see its demise. Some of his closest associates, like Egon Bahr, were downright hostile to it. But Brandt knew the distinction between state relations, which he was anxious to improve in the East, and a concern for societies, which he knew were still being repressed by their rulers, whatever the improvements.

Brandt was an old friend of Ernst (Ernie) Langendorf, an RFE public relations director for many years. He and Langendorf had been Social Democrats together in pre-Nazi Germany and had both fled the country in 1933. Langendorf eventually went to America and returned to Germany towards the end of the war with the U.S. army. He was apparently the first U.S. soldier to enter Munich. Whether this was a daring "recce" or a Harold Lloyd caper was never clarified, but Langendorf certainly dined out on it for years. More important, his friendship with Brandt revived. Although the two now met only rarely, they did so on one crucial occasion— when the *Ostpolitik* was underway. Langendorf asked Brandt what his government would do about RFE. Brandt, using his old familiar way of addressing Langendorf, replied, "Sir Ernst, we will do nothing."

What really deterred Brandt, and most of his Social Democrat colleagues, was the American protective relationship. A few left-wing Social Democrats were pro-Soviet, while many more were anti-Soviet but uneasy about American domination. They all knew their hands were tied by the Cold War. If, therefore, in the opinion of most Germans, any U.S. administration felt strongly about an issue or an institution, then it was hands off. And while the West German government presumably knew about the State Department's own reservations about RFE, they also knew that nobody in Washington wanted the Germans messing about with it. And in those days they cared.

In his book *In Europe's Name,* Timothy Garton Ash carries a short passage on Brandt's own cryptic record of a meeting with Gomułka during the German-Polish negotiations in December 1970 that sealed the success of West Germany's détente policy. The passage is worthy carrying in full.

Brandt records Gomułka asking, "What would a German court say if we sued Radio Free Europe?"

Brandt summarizes his own response thus, "Reference to overall development (?), relations with USA, possible changes through passing of time."

And then Gomułka, "But you give the license."

As Garton Ash says, "This does not sound like a very vigorous defence of RFE." True, but the key reference in Brandt's remarks is to "…. relations with the USA." That was his excuse, although he must have been a bit confounded by Gomułka's (perfectly correct) reference to the license. (It is just worth noting that a little earlier Garton Ash had described RFE's Polish Service—"Wolna Europa"— as "second to none" among the Western broadcasters.)

Larger and smaller examples of this restriction recurred throughout the Cold War. Perhaps the most popular centered on the Moscow Olympics in 1980, held less than one year after the Soviet invasion of Afghanistan. The U.S. Olympic Committee refused to go to Moscow, and the American government made it quietly clear that they expected unity from its allies on this point. But it did not get it. The British Olympic Committee, for example sent a team, as did the French. The Germans, however, although they obviously wanted to go, stayed home. And its Olympic committee left no doubt about why.

Helmut Schmidt, who succeeded Brandt in 1974, knew all about his country's overarching restrictions and accepted them. But he was considerably less gracious about it. This was evident in almost every facet of his relations with Washington, nowhere more so than in Schmidt's attitude to Radio Free Europe. In conversation with both colleagues and journalists, including RFE's own Bonn correspondent, the supremely knowledgeable Kurt de

Witt, he criticized the Radio as an obstacle to détente in general and an embarrassment to West Germany in particular. He thought nothing of bringing up the Radio in serious talks with American officials, among whom his *bête noir* in the Carter administration was undoubtedly Zbigniew Brzezinski, Polish-American and staunchly pro-RFE. Occasionally in his talks with Americans he would bring in RFE totally out of context. Forced into a corner during one argument, he yammered, "What about Radio Free Europe?"

What did the West German public think? After the Hungarian Revolution, it was strongly critical of RFE. But times do change. So did Germany and most Germans. Europe had changed, too. Even Radio Free Europe had changed. But the German public had not come to like RFE. They just stopped moaning about it; it had become part of the scenery. A young Hungarian editor once told a story that summed it all up. She came to work one day in a taxi. On arriving she paid and tipped the driver. He thanked her cheerfully, gave her a wink, and bade her "*Spioneren Sie gut!*" (Spy well!)

The Radio's Germans

RFE depended on the Germans in another, more intimate, way. It could not have lived for a day without its German staff. Studio technicians, medium-level engineers, junior newsroom staff, medium-level bureaucrats, secretarial staff, security, transport, cleaning, maintenance, and canteen personnel—they all added up to a full complement of about 250. Many of them had joined the Radio right at the beginning, not out of any flush of Western solidarity or anticommunist conviction, but because regular jobs in the incipient postwar German economy were scarce. Also, working for the Americans was counted a real privilege. Jobs at the numerous American military bases throughout southern Germany were eagerly sought after. The Americans paid better, too.

But it was more than just jobs and money. The works culture was different. The Americans treated their staff better, better than in the traditional Germanic culture of employer-employee relationships. You could now talk to your boss, and the traditional kowtowing was a thing of the past. Just politeness would do now. Labor relations at Radio Free Europe were in fact a tiny microcosm of the massive democratization of all those Germans lucky enough to live in West Germany.

The German staff did essential work and did it well. On the whole they were agreeable, even companionable, colleagues. Many had a rather superior, "Teutonic" attitude to their East European colleagues, but they normally kept it to themselves. Some developed a real, almost touching sense of loyalty to Radio Free Europe. As the West German economy surged forward, the German staff could often get better money outside. But many stuck with RFE. "It grows on you," one said to me.

4

New Beginnings—In Washington and Munich

The 1960s had brought a new look to RFE's leadership, both in New York and in Munich. In 1961, C. Rodney Smith had come to Munich as director. He was a former major general in the U.S. army and then a senior figure in American business. Smith knew nothing about Eastern Europe, but he was a firm and inspiring leader. He rallied the Radio in a remarkable way. One of his first achievements was to bring the topmost management of the Radio to Munich from New York.

Later in the 1960s, Ralph Walter assumed RFE's leadership in Munich and kept it for about fifteen years. He was a controversial character; but his single-minded dedication, steadfastness, energy, and reliability put everyone in his debt. It is difficult to imagine two human beings more dissimilar than Smith and Walter, but if RFE had a Pantheon, both would deserve prime places in it.

In Munich, R. V. (Dick) Burks eventually became policy director. Burks was the recent author of *The Dynamics of Communism in Eastern Europe*, a groundbreaking book that related the growth of communism in Eastern Europe to ethnic as well as economic questions. He began his RFE career as research director. A Broadcast Analysis Department was also set up. Its aim was to check programs more carefully—but still only *after* transmission. It was badly led, and its usefulness was limited. Research into East European problems was also strengthened. What had been a section now became a full department. The Central News Department also gained in staff and authority. Rodney Smith was determined that news and the objectivity of news should become among the most important elements in the Radio's entire output.

At the beginning of the 1960s I began to move on from my early duties of correcting the English of my exile colleagues. In the first real effort to strengthen RFE research and make it more objective—again a result of the 1956 debacle over Hungary—a number of specialist posts were created, mainly, but not solely, filled by Americans, to study each East European communist state more closely. I was given Romania and Bulgaria, the languages of which I began to learn, Romanian by a book, Bulgarian through a teacher. Later I became deputy director of Research and Analysis under Paul Collins.

It had not taken me long to realize what a decentralized operation Radio Free Europe actually was. The essentials of broadcast policy were laid down by the American policy leadership, but they were implemented independently by the five national Broadcast Services—Bulgarian, Czechoslovak, Hungarian, Polish, and Romanian. There was no central scripting. The Broadcast Services, therefore, enjoyed a remarkable degree of autonomy. Their political programming continued to be checked *after* not *before* broadcasting. This autonomy led to a vibrancy and a closer interaction with our audiences that would have been impossible under central scripting.

The central control that did exist at RFE lay in influencing the initiation of certain policy ideas, advice on the approach to them, and guidance on their implementation, as well as the setting of the parameters and constraints on them—all by the top American management. Getting things done at all depended on *trust*. It was trust that facilitated the emergence of a constructive coherence out of all the swirling centrifugal forces that existed at RFE—national, historical, cultural, educational, generational, social, professional, and departmental. It was trust that countered all these forces. These forces could brew and bubble up in the Radio canteen, in the corridors, and in private homes, but they were permanently barred from the Radio studios. Trust, of course did not come at once; it gestated over years. Without it Radio Free Europe's story would have been brief indeed.

This trust was apparently broken from time to time—but never, or hardly ever, deliberately. Misunderstanding, memory lapses, or just plain ignorance led to whatever lapses took place. I came to be convinced of this after many years of direct experience of the Radio. I still remain convinced.

The CIA and the "Need to Know" Psychology

It was Senator Clifford Case of New Jersey who finally and publicly blew the whistle about the CIA connection. He did this on the floor of the Senate in January 1971. It had certainly taken long enough. Most people in Washington, and many elsewhere, had known it for twenty years.

No doubt a crude deception had been practiced. As Case remarked, millions of Americans had been conned into contributing to the "Crusade for Freedom" believing that it was their dollars that enabled Radio Free Europe to broadcast to Eastern Europe. What actually made the Radio possible were the annual scores of millions from the Central Intelligence Agency.

At the Radio in Munich the link had been generally assumed. The CIA headquarters in Langley was known as the "pickle factory," its local agents as "the Friends." (Nothing to do with the Society of Friends). There was always a very small number of American employees (high and lowly) at the Radio in Munich who were seconded from the CIA. Among Americans and others at the Radio, the amateurish practice of initiating young American employees into the CIA "secret" was common knowledge. Initiates were made "witting" about the link and they were also warned that divulging the secret could mean a heavy fine or even a hefty jail sentence. That was ludicrous enough, but even sillier was the prescribed response of "No comment" to any questions from outside about a possible RFE connection with the CIA. Yet the "Need to Know" was a veritable mantra among the few who took their oath-taking seriously, those who "knew the name of the game." (Again, clichés abounded). It seemed childish and bizarre in a broadcasting station extolling the virtues of open government to communist-ruled audiences.

Most RFE employees sensibly shrugged off the CIA connection; they had more important things to worry about. After all, somebody had to finance the station and the American government was a worthy institution. The CIA, too, supported many worthy causes. And there *was* a war going on—"cold" at the moment, but who knew? But there were also some employees, mainly senior Americans, whose mentality got an undoubted kick out of the CIA link. They were "in the know" and liked to think that this made them special. For them knowing "the name of the game" was patriotically consoling. Some exiles, too, had developed a psychology that relished secrecy and conspiracy. One Czechoslovak editor once darkly warned a colleague "that Jim Brown (me) was working for the British." "Poor bloody British" was her uplifting response.

Many had assumed that it was only a matter of time before the whistle was blown. But some "believing" Americans had strongly felt that the CIA link could, and should, continue indefinitely. The Cold War was on, the CIA was an essential element in it, and so was Radio Free Europe. It was, therefore, the patriotic duty of Congress to understand and accept this. Not to do so was, if not an act of betrayal, then clear enough evidence of dangerously subversive thinking. The "Spirit of the Sixties" in the United States and in Western Europe became incomprehensible for such believers. The growing opposition to the Vietnam War, the student revolts in 1968, the first big signs of basic polarization in America—"No Comment" was somehow out of tune in an avalanche like this. Some drastic reorganization was needed.

Enter the BIB

The reorganization came after laborious governmental study and deliberation, and menacing senatorial investigations in which Senator J. William Fulbright, an avowed enemy of both RFE and Radio Liberty, played the dominating role. But what Fulbright's Senate hearings showed, much to his chagrin, was that a large number of people in American public life wanted RFE to continue. The Radio's staff was grateful for the support it got and reassured by it. What emerged when all the dust settled was the Board for International Broadcasting (BIB). It was to have a supervisory role over both RFE and Radio Liberty, which was also based in Munich broadcasting to the Soviet Union. Open U.S. government financing, approved by the Congress, should be channeled through the BIB to the two radios. The president would appoint BIB members, five in all. The BIB would also have a small, permanent executive staff. Links between the CIA and the Radios were officially cut.

This reorganization was a mixed blessing. It saved Radio Free Europe; there can be no doubt about that. But it also involved the administrative merging of RFE with Radio Liberty (RL). RFE, therefore, disappeared as a distinct institution. Administratively, there was something to be said for this merger. Considerable amounts of money were saved, especially when RL moved entirely into the RFE Munich building in 1976. It was a tight fit but the operation was managed admirably.

Psychologically, though, the merger caused difficulties from the start. RFE broadcast to the East European nations whose states were forcibly ruled by the Soviet Union, which after World War II had also helped itself to some of their territories. Furthermore, except for Bulgaria, the East European nations, as represented in Radio Free Europe, hated Russia, "the inhuman land," and thoroughly despised the Russians. As for the Russians, precommunist, communist, and anticommunist, they in their turn generally despised the East Europeans. In particular, nearly all of them hated the Poles. For their part, the Poles regarded this hatred as yet further proof of their international superiority.

These historical antipathies were, to some extent, reflected in the newly established "RFE/RL." Many Radio Liberty staff, including even some of the non-Russians, regarded their RFE counterparts as trumped-up poseurs, broadcasting to pipsqueak countries, certainly not worth the money being spent on them. As for the RFE staff, most regarded their Russian colleagues as either near or over the border of barbarism and were totally bemused by some of RL's Asian nationalities. Early on in the merger, there was the story, one hoped apocryphal, of an RFE Pole, London-educated, going into the canteen and finding it virtually full of RL staff. He spotted another Pole at the far end of the canteen, went up to him, shook his hand and said "Dr. Livingstone, I presume."

At first the Board for International Broadcasting seemed a good idea, even "a tribute to the American political genius," as one American, seriously, not satirically, put it to me. In its working, however, the BIB hardly lived up to expectations. In the first place, its successive members were, with one or two exceptions, plainly mediocre. Much more important, the BIB, mostly driven by its permanent executive staff, sought to establish not just supervision but total dominance over RFE/RL's Munich management. The result was a series of all-too-familiar, unedifying, "turf wars" that the Munich management almost invariably lost.

The prime personal responsibility for this lay with Walter Roberts, the head of BIB's permanent staff. Roberts was an able, intelligent man, author of a fine book on Tito's Yugoslavia, who had also been the most senior foreign-born executive ever in the United States Information Agency (USIA). He was the bureaucrat's bureaucrat. In what he saw as a personal battle between himself and the Munich management, he lost no opportunity to denigrate it. He invariably supported the State Department in its pressure against RFE programming. It was Roberts who was at least partially responsible for suggesting that, under the rubric of détente, Radio Free Europe should change its name to "Radio Dialogue" and give the East European communist regimes "the right of reply" to RFE programs they objected to—this in RFE airtime and at U.S. taxpayers' expense. These ideas were soon forgotten, but they caused much concern, incredulity, and fury while they remained subjects for "serious" discussion.

The Scare over Portugal

A noteworthy episode in RFE's history had passed two years earlier, in 1974. It resulted from the "Carnation Revolution" in Portugal, where a number of younger army officers had ousted the regime of Marcello Caetano, ending nearly fifty years of fascist rule. Portugal was of more than passing interest to the Radio because the bulk of its transmitters were located there. If they were closed, then RFE was dead, and for a time it looked highly likely that this would happen. On a visit I made to Washington during that time, one National Security Council bigwig assured me that we could "kiss those transmitters goodbye."

The new Portuguese government appointed a certain Captain Rosa to be its "advisory officer" concerning RFE. He subsequently came to Munich to look over RFE's facilities. Captain Rosa was visibly impressed by what he saw. Apparently he had expected just "a few Nissan-huts with the odd transmitter or two." His amiable personality did something to soothe our nerves. He later went to Washington for more senior-level talks, and eventually the new government decided to leave the transmitters where they were.

Why? It was obviously not just the good impression we made on Captain Rosa, or simply that the Carnation revolutionaries were glad of the rent RFE paid for the transmitters. It was partly because the new government in Lisbon was anxious to show that it was not as left wing as the world was thinking. And—closely linked—it had no desire to offend the United States unnecessarily. Its decision and the motives for it were, therefore, similar to those of the new Brandt SPD government in West Germany in 1970. (See chapter 3.)

The New Generation

Generational change profoundly affected the composition of RFE's staff in Munich as well as its style of broadcasting. At its foundation most of its staff were drawn from the newly established exile political parties in the West. Many of its members were highly educated, estimable men (women editors were thin on the ground). Some of them made good broadcasters, but almost all looked backwards. The future Eastern Europe should conform to what they had known in the past.

The defeat of the Hungarian Revolution led to the first gradual influx, however small, of new RFE members. Younger refugees gradually replaced aging "founding fathers." Relations between the two groups inevitably tended to be strained. Some of the new recruits were tactful and adaptable; others were arrogant and "disrespectful." They were also generally from a social class or two lower than their established colleagues, who contended that even after such a short exposure to communism they had become morally and ideologically tainted by it. After the Soviet invasion of Czechoslovakia, similar difficulties occurred. A few of the new Czechoslovak staff additions had previously been high fliers on the Czech radio during the Prague Spring. In their different ways they were real professionals; but despite their radio expertise (or because of it) they got a generally cold, sometimes even hostile, welcoming. The RFE Poles changed more gradually, and such was the numerical strength of the Polish postwar emigration that new staff members could often be selected from it. But in the late seventies new faces, fresh from Poland, did appear and were absorbed relatively quietly, although one long-standing Polish staff member periodically bewailed to me that the new arrivals had a "totally different mentality."

But the most profound, often overlooked difference between the generations was in world and cultural outlook. RFE's "founder" generation was totally European. That meant not anti-American, but un-American. The founders came from upper-class families throughout the East European region. They grew up in a world and a continent dominated, and fought over, by European powers. America was a far-off country of which they had known little and probably cared less. America was a place to which peasants and Jews emigrated, very few indeed of their own. In world politics, though it won World War I in Europe, America then chose fatefully to withdraw from it. Culturally, too, Europe was the center of gravity. Paris, especially, but also Berlin, London, and Rome were the places that mattered.

But then came World War II, with America emerging as by far the greatest Western power. It immediately became locked in the Cold War with the Soviet behemoth that had ravaged their own countries and their civilization. They were grateful to America for the succor it was giving them. But they had been formed in a quite different culture, and this certainly showed at Radio Free Europe.

The next generations at RFE often had connections with America through relatives who had emigrated there. Some of them were also from families that had benefited from the social mobility that communism generated. Some had also been Communist Party members and had no affection whatever for the classes they had displaced. Ideologically they had been inculcated with anti-Americanism. But their fascination with America increased as their disillusionment with communism and their disdain for the Soviet Union deepened. What became clearer to them with every passing day was that it was America, once the "forbidden fruit," that represented the genuine "new," and offered the true opportunities. Hence, when the lucky few eventually found their way to Radio

Free Europe, they may not have been Jeffersonian democrats, but they were on their way to being full-fledged pro-Americans, more genuinely so than most of their older colleagues. Culturally, too, they looked over Europe towards America. In short, they respected Europe but admired, even wondered at, America.

5

Approaches, Attitudes, Audiences

I never knew much about broadcasting. A strange confession, perhaps, for an RFE director. But I soon developed views on what should go into broadcasting, and what should not. What follows is what I felt most strongly about, either way.

What Not to Do

Those directing RFE had to be aware of the historic "elite culture" of the East European exile, especially the Polish exile, and while duly admiring it had to be determined to ignore it. It was a worthy culture and could be inspiring, but now it could also lead to a serious lack of realism. The historical links between exile and homeland had been almost exclusively *links between elites*. Most of Radio Free Europe's staff, especially its core staff, recruited immediately after the communist seizure of power, came from the social and intellectual elites of their nations. But RFE's broadcasts were aimed at *all sections* of the East European populations; it had a *mass* audience. The time when intellectuals could pride themselves as embodying the spirit of the nation had passed. It was time for some perspective and a little humility. What was needed now was professionalism, not pretentiousness.

Professionalism began to appear in strength at Radio Free Europe in the 1960s. For me one of the most gratifying things about working at the Radio was beginning to hear outside journalists, scholars, and broadcasters praise our work as "professional." We were indeed crossing the divide from romanticism to realism.

Attendant on this tradition was the danger of overrating ourselves and underrating our audiences. Most of our listeners were uneducated (at least in the formal sense), but they were far from gullible. They were suspicious of everybody and everything. That included Radio Free Europe. The only way to mitigate this deep divide was through a combination of honesty, accuracy, modesty, and again, a touch of humility. Self-importance, "talking down," and pompousness had to be resisted and routed.

Another danger to avoid was assuming that our audiences were as interested in us as we were in them. Again it was a matter of perspective and modesty. This is not to say that East Europeans had better things to do than listen to Radio Free Europe, but that they had more important, urgent things to do. Staying alive for example, or coping with the never-ending grind and grayness of life under communism. The Radio was not an integral part of their life but an adjunct to it. Our programs had to be geared to that reality. The more they were, the more important an adjunct we would become.

RFE broadcasters also had to accept that in no circumstances was it their job to be promoting disorder. Many Westerners, of course, suspected that this was precisely what RFE broadcasters did do. The truth was that RFE could never have fomented disorder even had it tried to; and after 1956 it never tried to. Many, though, thought that it not only could do but should do so. Frank Shakespeare, head of the Board for International Broadcasting during the Reagan era, said in an interview shortly before he took that post that RFE should be fomenting strikes. Ben Wattenberg, his deputy, told me in 1982 that we should "start ratcheting things up." There were some in RFE itself, of course, who thought the same. They chafed at the restrictions placed on them, convinced that they could stir up strikes if only they were allowed to. They just had to be curbed.

To Be *For* Something

Finally — and most important of all — Radio Free Europe had to show its listeners and the world outside that it should not just be *against* something—communism, but also *for* something — democracy. We had to convey through all possible means that democracy was the only legitimation for any state or government. And we had to keep both ourselves and our audiences aware that we were anticommunist because we were democratic; we were not necessarily democratic because we were anticommunist. (With its operational headquarters in Munich, of all places, there was no excuse for forgetting that). All well and good, of course, but conveying democracy was not as simple at RFE as it sounded. It had to keep in mind that very few of its staff of whatever generation (interwar Czechoslovaks generally excepted) had any experience of democracy. Most East Europeans were historically more nationalist than democratic. And some of RFE's original staff—Hungarians, Slovaks, Romanians, and Bulgarians—had fought for, or supported, Nazi Germany in World War II.

Obviously such circumstances made RFE's democratizing task all the more daunting. I felt touched and honored when a splendid old Bulgarian, a prewar diplomat, once suggested to me that I give his countrymen at the Radio, including himself, a course in "democracy." I demurred as humbly as I could, telling him that it was through the whole Western democratic ambience at RFE that democracy was best imparted. I also remember insisting to him that democracy must always be considered an aspiration, never an achievement. Once it came to be regarded as an achievement, it was already in decline. I tried—rather falteringly, I admit—to make this my "credo" in Munich. It disconcerted some of my colleagues, mostly Americans. But even after a long period of rustication and retirement, I obstinately maintain that I was right.

(Incidentally, the "splendid old Bulgarian" I have just mentioned pointed out to me one of RFE's historical ironies. Bulgarians lived for nearly 500 years of their history under "the Turkish Yoke." Yet now, every workday evening in Radio Free Europe in Munich, Turkish Gastarbeiter cleaners were cleaning out its Bulgarian Service offices and lavatories. He was not vindictive about it, just wry).

A Plan for the Eighties

In September 1977, when I was deputy director of RFE, I put down some thoughts on future programming in a memo to my boss, Director Bill Buell, a good man to work for. I think we also shared many opinions, and many values too. I only rediscovered this memo in 2004; my friend Ross Johnson sent me a copy. It had been immortalized at the Hoover Institution at Stanford University. Now, at a distance of nearly thirty years, its ideas still seem presentable, even if two of its closely linked premises were monumentally wrong. One pertained to the world situation, the other to the situation within Radio Free Europe itself. It assumed an indefinite continuation of the Soviet Union and its will and ability to retain its hegemony in Eastern Europe. Within the Radio itself, it assumed a broad continuation of its post-1956 philosophy of accepting communist control in Eastern Europe and seeking to change it, radically, by evolutionary means. I am not ashamed for having been wrong.

Following are sections of my September 1977 memo [which ends on page 68 below]:

Influence as Well as Audience

The uniqueness of RFE lies in the fact that it has influence as well as audience. By influence is meant an ability to take part in the course of political development. This ability varies considerably from country to country, and even where it is at its greatest it should not be exaggerated. But it is the existence of this capacity that distinguishes RFE from other Western stations broadcasting to Eastern Europe. (It should be noted that I am using influence in a *specific* sense here: obviously anything that is listened to has influence of some kind, even if indirect, subconscious, or subliminal; but few radio stations have ever had the sort of influence RFE has always exercised.)

It is this influence that makes RFE controversial and disliked by the East European regimes and by many American diplomats. It is this influence that makes the East European regime leaderships quite right, from their point of view, when they accuse us of continuous interference in their internal affairs. The point here is that the continuing existence of RFE is based and justified only on the premise that a sharp differentiation can still be made between state and society in Eastern Europe. Once this differentiation disappears, or begins to disappear, as it seemed to be doing in Czechoslovakia in 1968, then RFE ceases to be legitimate.

Many of the suggestions made in recent years for emasculating RFE programming have been consciously or unconsciously aimed at removing this influence. Some who have advanced these suggestions have been clear-sightedly aware that once that influence was gone, RFE's *raison d'etre* would go, too. This would be a less direct and messy way of putting an end to its operations than the one formerly advocated by Senator William Fulbright. Others seem genuinely to have believed that we could function perfectly as a kind of "neutral information radio." This is palpably mistaken. We could not do so for several reasons, one of the most important being that very many of our listeners are attracted to us precisely because of that quality or dimension in our broadcasting that tends to give us influence. RFE is not as other stations are! If we tried to be this, it would be perceived very quickly and would be ascribed—quite correctly—to political restrictions. Our audience figures would suffer drastically. We would soon become useless, unworthy of support, ready for closure. In this sense we are a prisoner of our influence.

I should make clear right away that I am in no way advocating "Cold War," aggressive broadcasting. Nor do I have any sympathy whatever with those who argue that "concessionist" political restrictions have already reduced our influence. Indeed I feel that some of our broadcasting is still too aggressive or too intent on scoring petty debating points; on rare occasions it is downright crude. I think more sophisticated broadcasting on domestic affairs, a more judicious selection of Western topics—to mention just two areas where improvements could be made—would enhance and sharpen our influence, make us more a force to be reckoned with in Eastern Europe. I return to this subject later.

Varying Degrees of Influence

I have already said that this influence varies from country to country; but extent of influence is not to be confused with size of audience. RFE's highest percentage audience is in Romania, but I very much doubt whether RFE's influence is as high in Romania as it is in Poland. RFE's Romanian broadcasting tends to mirror the often deplorable facts of public life in Romania. Many of its broadcasts on domestic subjects feed and focus the public's dismay with the current situation. Some of its broadcasts also provide an individual "listener's complaint service": the very successful "Listeners' Mail" programs on individual cases of family reunion, those who wish to emigrate, and others. (There is no denying RFE's effectiveness here. But success in enabling people to get out of the country is a distinctive and rather narrow example of influence on the domestic scene). The Romanian Service's spectacularly successful service to listeners after last winter's [1976–77] earthquake was certainly RFE's most outstanding broadcasting ever of this kind.

Our impact in Poland is different. The Polish Service is an external but active participant in the ebb and flow of public life in Poland. It is a factor of which the regime must take note before embarking on any major policy innovation. It has certainly had some (beneficial) influence on regime decisions over the last two decades, although the extent of this influence cannot be measured. Take, for example, the Polish leadership's pressure on the regime in July [1977] to apply the general amnesty to the nine intellectuals and five workers still in prison. No one in his right mind would claim that the Polish Service's pressure was mainly responsible for this. But few would deny that its policy of continually keeping the issue before its audience was a considerable factor in the general pressure that finally persuaded the Gierek leadership to show leniency. Indeed, RFE can claim this episode as an important success for its broadcasting policy.

There has been considerable criticism of this policy on the grounds that the Polish Service was "overdoing" the human rights issue. There were those who felt that "pushing" this issue too much would harm rather than help the people concerned. In this particular case they were wrong and, both morally and politically, RFE's policy of pressure was vindicated. (This is not to say that a policy of pressure will always be the right one. Sometimes caution or silence, which our critics were advocating in the Polish case this summer, will in fact be necessary.)

The direct influence of the other three Broadcast Services has been much less apparent, although it would be mistaken to conclude that it has not existed. In the case of Hungary in 1956, RFE's influence was disastrous. During the long, slow process of development that led up to the Prague Spring, RFE's Czechoslovak Service undoubtedly exerted some influence of a most beneficial kind. Today our influence in both these countries is probably slight: in Czechoslovakia because of the persisting political apathy dating from 1968, in Hungary because of the "benevolence" of Kádár's rule. The task of both these services now is to retain audience and credibility. The situation in Czechoslovakia cannot go on as it is indefinitely; when some semblance of political life or movement begins again, there will be adequate scope for our influence to be felt. Equally in Hungary, Kádár's leadership cannot continue forever, and the question "Can Kádárism survive Kádár?" is already being asked. The post-Kádár uncertainty or even instability will present the Hungarian Service with a real opportunity to play a small but historic role in Hungarian public life. As it is, it can go on urging a widening and deepening of reforms already made.

RFE's influence in Bulgaria remains an unknown quantity. In my view, over the last ten–twelve years or so, the Bulgarian Service has provided constructive, well-documented, and informative programming. But this period has coincided with one of impressive political stability and economic growth in Bulgaria—hardly a situation conducive to the exertion of influence by an external radio station. But there is every reason to believe that in the next few years Bulgaria will not escape the instability that will affect

Eastern Europe. Then I am convinced that the patient work of the Bulgarian Service over the last few years will pay off. The credibility it has built up will bear fruit in the form of real influence.

The retention of credibility during periods of stability in Eastern Europe, when opportunities for the exertion of perceptible influence practically do not exist, is a task whose importance cannot be exaggerated. Our degree of influence in periods of crisis is closely correlated with our degree of credibility in periods of stability.

The Need for an Informed Public Opinion

A decisive element for change in Eastern Europe is an informed, alert public opinion. All the regimes, if in varying degrees, have become more responsive over the last two decades to pressure from below. Pressure can be exercised either violently through rebellion or peacefully through knowledge. The regimes have come to realize that they cannot mislead societies that know what is going on in their own countries, in other communist-ruled countries, and in the rest of the world.

To keep public opinion informed and, therefore, alert continues to be an important task. I do not consider it "disruptive" to do so as our critics, in both East and West, maintain. The disruptive factor in Eastern Europe is not RFE, Helsinki [Conference on Security and Cooperation in Europe], Eurocommunism, or the like, but Soviet hegemony and communist rule. Anything that blunts that hegemony, that makes that rule less inconsonant with both human dignity and the legitimate desires of people, will tend to reduce the dangers of those periodic explosions in Eastern Europe that have caused serious suffering and increased international tension. If an informed, alert public opinion does that, then the greatest single factor in making it alert and informed (namely, Radio Free Europe) deserves better than to be dismissed as an "inciting center."

The objection will be raised that what really counts in

the power situation we are in is not *our* perceptions but those of the East European regimes and, particularly, that of the Soviet Union. The peaceful Prague Spring was, after all, followed by August 1968, and there is no guarantee that the same would not happen again. This is a serious objection, and its gravity and implications should be weighed all the more earnestly by an organization like ours, working outside the countries concerned. But to be dominated totally by this ever-possible danger would be to accept paralysis. The East Europeans would have to resign themselves to paralysis, and so would RFE. The former would consider it too dangerous to press for any improvement of their lot; RFE, knowing that informed citizens are the most likely to press for changes, would have to cease operation. And the dynamics of the East European situation make it unrealistic for anyone concerned (including RFE) to think in terms of a limited or finite set of improvements—just so far and no further. Once change begins in Eastern Europe its course is indeterminate. There can be no saying "We just want this and no more." Progress is dynamic.

Aiming at Different Sections

RFE should direct its effort, with more focus, planning, and resources than before, on that huge and growing stratum of East European society known as the *intelligentsia*, including the more narrowly defined creative intellectuals. It is this stratum that can exert by far the greatest influence for peaceful, institutional change; it is this stratum that tends to straddle the divide between state and society in Eastern Europe; it is this stratum that is more amenable to the reach and influence of Western radio.

The *working class* is, of course, the one most capable of producing direct, immediate results. This was shown most dramatically in Poland in 1970 and 1976. Even in Romania, whose leadership is often considered the least responsive to public opinion, a miners' strike in the Jiu Valley in 1976 could make Ceauşescu interrupt his vacation. Throughout

Eastern Europe, often at the local level, sometimes at the national, regime policies are modified in response to worker opposition. Why not, therefore, concentrate our efforts on the workers? There are two obvious reasons why not: (1) worker pressure is the one most likely to lead to physical confrontation and bloodshed; (2) Western radio's capacity to influence workers is smaller (keep in mind, we could not start strikes even if we tried to). Finally, the results usually produced by successful worker pressure on the regimes seldom lead to the kind of institutional change that must take place if evolutionary progress in Eastern Europe is to be secure. Workers' pressure almost always leads to material improvements—to "consumerism." These are essential, but they are no substitute for institutional change, except in the eyes of the regimes and the Soviet Union. The incipient institutional reform brought about by the intelligentsia in Eastern Europe in the sixties would have led to fundamental change. Consumerism as practiced in the seventies is a major weapon used by the communist leaderships to fight off fundamental change.

A word about the *peasantry*. Despite industrialization, this is still a stratum of major political importance. But it hardly seems destined to engineer major political change in most of Eastern Europe in the foreseeable future. Where there is collectivized agriculture—i.e., everywhere but Poland—the peasantry cannot be considered "badly off" in East European terms, except in Romania. In Hungary and Czechoslovakia, indeed, they are prosperous. The desire to return to private ownership is still present, but it is not as great as it was, and in many cases hardly constitutes a major pressure on the regimes. It is only in Poland, so often the exception, that the peasantry seems likely to mount a serious challenge to the regime, given certain conditions. These would exist if the regime put a speedy socialization drive into effect, and a rural alliance between private farmers and Catholic clergy could then form which could result in violent Jacquerie-type confrontation. It would certainly offer passive resistance involving the refusal to meet delivery targets. The subsequent shortages in the towns would inevitably lead to worker discontent, perhaps degenerating into violence. But even without a socialization threat peasant dissatisfaction over procurement prices could result in lower or irregular supplies to the towns, producing some degree of discontent. Directly or indirectly, therefore, the Polish peasantry could become a destabilising force but hardly one promoting peaceful institutional change over the nation as a whole.

The Dissidents

It is to the intelligentsia that one must turn, therefore, as the main carrier of reform. In this context there are two groups of the intelligentsia—"dissident" and "nonconformist"— that are of most interest to RFE.

Taking the *dissidents* first, their importance in East European history remains to be seen. In several countries, as in the Soviet Union, they have already inflicted major moral defeats on the regimes, and in Poland a serious political defeat also. At present there is a general lull in dissident activity throughout the region, but if predictions of instability in Eastern Europe—which I, among others, have made—turn out to be true, dissidents are likely to become a regular feature of the political scene, small in number but a serious challenge because of their exertions, their example, and the publicity they receive. RFE should give supportive publicity to all dissident activities that are within the laws of the country concerned except when it becomes clear that this publicity is a direct cause of regimes' vindictiveness against them. (Usually RFE publicity has helped dissidents, notably in Poland in July.) RFE should not, however, intervene directly in dissidents' activities by urging the rest of the population to support them, by giving addresses, phone numbers, etc. It should be selective in the dissident documents it broadcasts.

The dissident movement is closely linked with the whole issue of human rights. Human rights are what this radio stands for: we propagate and defend them. But differences can arise—have already arisen—about how much radio time we should give to human rights. For, though it is a many-faceted issue, it has not yet directly affected the majority of inhabitants in any of the East European countries. It would obviously be a serious mistake, therefore, so to load our programs with human rights material that we give the impression that this is the audience country's only preoccupation. (Sometimes both the Polish and Romanian Services have tended to do this). On the other hand, it would be a serious mistake to determine the extent of our programming on human rights by counting the numbers involved or affected. For reasons too obvious to enumerate it (the principle of human rights) must get more time than its mere arithmetic might prescribe.

Nonconformists: The Hope for the Future

But with all admiration for the dissidents, it is the nonconformist intelligentsia with whom the best hopes lie for peaceful, institutional reform. These are the educated "regimists" who have "evolved" into nonconformism. They occupy important or potentially important places in the economy, the state administration, education, and culture. Most are Party members. They are well treated by the regime in terms of position, perks, material goods, travel abroad, etc. They have many vested interests in the perpetuation of the present system. They are part of the Establishment. But, this aside, they have little in common with the real ruling elite, which is the party *apparat*, the security *apparat*, and the officer corps. They are not fully trusted by this elite, whom they increasingly despise, but are perceived as necessary to it. In fact, their influence on a large area of decision-making is increasing.

Most of these characteristics apply to the intelligentsia as a whole outside the fringe group of dissidents, to conformists as well as nonconformists. What distinguishes the nonconformists is often a quiet, growing, sympathy with the dissidents' underlying beliefs, although they may have little sympathy for the dissidents' persons or methods. They often listen to Western radio; this includes RFE, although many of them would hesitate to own up to it. They are interested in Western ideas, trends, and developments— economic, political, social, and intellectual. They are concerned about Western problems and difficulties too, for they know that tomorrow these will be theirs also. They want more direct contact with the West. They are attracted to Eurocommunism. They are cynical about Marxism-Leninism; some are cynical about everything. They see that their national economies and scientific-technical development have long reached a point where the command structure becomes counterproductive. They want economic reform along the lines of the sixties but going further. They know that its corollary is greater pluralism in public life as a whole. They want this too.

Our aim here should be twofold: to attract more of these people to our audience; and to induce as many conformists as possible to join the ranks of the nonconformists.

Some Proposals

How can we do this? Part of the answer has just been supplied when enumerating some of the nonconformists' interests. We should have more varied programming on the whole range of Western topics. We concentrate too much on political affairs, too little on social and intellectual topics. Here the Central News Department could do more. More items of social and intellectual interest should be put in the news. More features should deal with nonpolitical developments. Political developments are often covered better by experts writing on them in the elite Western press. More press features on nonpolitical topics in the West should go into the news files.

Part of the answer lies in the Research Department's supplying an even greater range of East European cross-reporting and Eurocommunist material. It also lies in more of the objectivity and restraint that characterize the research product also being reflected in programming. Obviously, the spoken word is different from the written. Programming must contain those dimensions of color, personality, and "snap" that have no place in research material. But I am convinced that, in spite of the improvements in broadcasting that have undoubtedly taken place, more restraint, less harping, fewer generalizations, less driving home the obvious, fewer adjectives, less polemicizing with party editorials, more writing for the gratification of the listener rather than the writer—all this would step up our appeal to this vital section of the audience.

I would also recommend more program planning than appears to exist at present. I am well aware that a whole subjective and objective range of difficulties militates against even short-term planning. So does shortage of money. I know also that much of radio broadcasting has to consist of the spontaneous, response to the present, the ephemeral. But this can, and does, often serve as an excuse for haphazardness, lack of planning, lack of purpose. Why is this script being written? What impact is it designed to have?

As I have already mentioned, the next few years could well be a time of marked instability in Eastern Europe. This instability could be serious, resulting in explosive violence. But it could be the kind of instability conducive to the initiation of change, the accelerator of developments offering real hope for a better future in Eastern Europe. We must be ready for this.

These then, were my thoughts and predictions in September 1977. They were not untypical for those who thought seriously about Eastern Europe. Their biggest misjudgment was about the Soviet Union's future—also not untypical for those who thought seriously about Eastern Europe. But my underestimation of the impact that workers' strikes could have in Poland was just bad analysis. The institutional impact of the Polish strikes and the formation of Solidarity made nonsense of it.

RFE's "Other Audience"

After having discussed the key segments of RFE's audience it is now appropriate to recall that it had another audience, too. No one in Eastern Europe listened to RFE's programs more assiduously than the regime officials themselves. The Radio's political programs were monitored and copies of them prepared for Politburo members in all five target countries. Not only that: *evaluations* of RFE programs were also made; changes of emphasis were noted, shifts of judgment, new programs, perceived RFE changes in tactics and strategy. No doubt, RFE was taken seriously.

Some East European observers have subsequently argued that, by concentrating on certain topics, RFE could unconsciously "do the regimes' work for them." For example, RFE "made Ceauşescu in the sixties and early seventies," so the argument goes. It reported extensively on Romania's "independence" policy first under Gheorghiu-Dej and then, after 1965, under Ceauşescu. But it was not so much the reports as the comments on Romanian policy that were key. The Romanian regime media did report some aspects of Bucharest's foreign policy, but they could hardly comment on what it meant, what it involved. RFE was saying or implying that various aspects of Romanian policy, indeed the policy as a whole, were anti-Soviet. In its press reviews RFE was also quoting the world's press saying the same thing. Hence it was doing what the official Bucharest media could not do themselves. The Bucharest regime was probably attempting to deny constantly to Moscow that its policy was anti-Soviet, yet it was more than happy for RFE to say exactly the opposite to the Romanian people.

According to some Hungarian listeners, RFE also helped the Kádár regime, if in a different context. It reported, for example, Kádár's reluctance to join in the invasion of Czechoslovakia in August 1968 and his alleged personal warning to Dubček about the seriousness of his situation. On the home front, where the Soviet post-Khrushchev agenda was obviously not reform but reaction, RFE praised those reforms in Hungary that were still continuing and later greatly expanded. Obviously, this had to be left unsaid by the Kádár regime itself. Hence it was good to have someone saying it to the Hungarian people, telling them that at least the regime was trying. And there was no one better to do this than Kádár's old enemy, Radio Free Europe.

6

News and Research

The News and the Research operations were the two pillars of Radio Free Europe's reliability and became internationally respected. They both deserve a closer look.

News

First, staffing: Among a total journalistic staff of up to thirty were several Americans, as well as several Australians recruited almost entirely from international news agencies in London. Almost the entire staff were newsmen, that is, news desk or "slot" editors. Some, like Iain MacDonald and Roly Eggleston, evolved into special correspondents, mainly for ongoing international meetings like the Conference on Security and Cooperation in Europe (CSCE). The professional standard of the newsroom was high. Some of its editors were recognized as "world standard." They all had political views of their own, which after working hours they were not slow in airing. But in the "slot" they were totally neutral. News, of course, could be slanted by selection, but there is no evidence that this was ever done consciously. Sometimes during my own years at the Radio I heard the Australians being branded as a "left-wing lot." It was a specious generalization.

The News Room was by far the biggest element in the News Department. It operated twenty-four hours a day. The overnight shift was tiny, but often it had to work on some of the most important international breaking stories. Day and night the News Room shifts prepared crisp, Western-style news items in the English language. Its news items were then passed on to the five Broadcast Service newsrooms, which then prepared hourly newscasts based on them.

There was sometimes pressure from successive directors of the News Department for a standard RFE hourly newscast, the same for all five Broadcast Services, to be translated and then broadcast. The Radio management wisely rejected this idea on the grounds that different national audiences were not all interested in the same things. Obviously all five Broadcast Services were expected to carry the most important international news, but then they could pick and choose according to their audience's concerns and interests. The job of Central News was to provide a full enough "menu" for all five Broadcast Services to be satisfied.

Shortly after the Hungarian Revolution the two-source rule was introduced into the News Room. Every item of news had to be backed by two sources.

The two-source decision was at first strongly objected to by some of the Broadcast Service directors, led by Jan Nowak. Their argument was that occasionally they, the service directors, were informed by a reliable source from their own countries of a news development that obviously merited newscast inclusion. But the two-source rule meant that, however reliable a source might be, or reputed to be, his (or her) item of news could not be used till confirmed by another source. Such confirmation usually occurred very soon if the story was true. Still, a certain amount of time was lost. It was safety against speed, better right than first.

There were, of course, dodges to get around the spirit of the two-source rule. For example, the News Room got a story from, say Nowak, then called Reuters and AP in London about the story; they would then check with their correspondents in Warsaw. Very soon Reuters and AP in Warsaw carried the story and there were the two sources! But Reuters and AP would only bother to check the story because of the credibility that RFE enjoyed among professional newsmen in Eastern Europe.

Some of RFE's exile staff would get impatient with the News Room. "They know bugger-all about Eastern Europe," one irate Czech once exploded to me. He was quite right about most of them. But subject expertise was not paramount in News. What did matter were intelligence, experience, and professionalism. RFE News had those in abundance, and the proof was in the acknowledged excellence and reliability of the newscasts. In fact RFE's audience for news shot up at times of crisis. Only with a rigorously enforced Western practice could the News Room's reputation have been achieved and maintained.

The standards of *serious* Western journalism never ceased to amaze me. A professional journalist from, say, the *New York Times*, would be sent on a two-week tour of Eastern Europe. He (or she) would usually first come to RFE Munich for a couple of days' briefing and then was off. The quality of the ensuing reportage was highly impressive. Naturally, a *New York Times* correspondent had red-carpet treatment everywhere, eventually even in Eastern Europe. Still, it was the discernment of the reporting that was so striking, its speed plus a quality the Germans used to call *souverän*.

The RFE News Room's most impressive output was the "Budget" (an American expression, apparently, for the total product of a News Department). It included not only the News Room's own news items (on white paper) but also the news reports, articles, editorials, and analyses from almost the entire Western press—American, British, French, German, Italian, Swiss, Scandinavian, and occasionally Spanish (on buff paper). Over a twenty-four-hour period this came to at least a five-inch-thick load of reading. In a sort of "sub-Budget" there was also a lengthy series of items pertaining to culture, media, sport, cinema, and the theatre (on blue paper). My old friend Arthur Breslauer was in charge of the blue items. RFE wives, in particular, were grateful to him.

The RFE Budget was a truly astonishing product. About eighty of the total RFE staff were "entitled" to receive the Budget, which was collected from pigeonholes at one end of the News Room. Being on the delivery list was a matter of prestige within the Radio. The News Room could be irritatingly selective about entitlement, and sometimes ill feeling arose in the different departments over who got the Budget and who didn't.

Not surprisingly the Budget presented a huge problem of selective reading. To read *one* day's Budget carefully took *several* days. At the beginning of his RFE career one of my colleagues used to spend more than half the day on less than half the Budget.

He tried to read everything. He didn't last long. Experience and ruthlessness helped selectivity, but even a relatively conscientious reader was occasionally caught out having missed or skipped a key item. What followed was public humiliation at the daily morning policy meetings attended by policy staff, Broadcast Service directors, representatives of News, Research, and Audience Research, and Radio guests. RFE's director or policy director usually presided over these meetings. They established, sometimes after considerable arguments, the broadcast policy line to be taken on the main Eastern and Western news of the day.

Monitoring

Radio monitoring, dour, dull, and too often unnoticed, was an essential supplement to news. It was RFE's closest thing to the proverbial "rock face." The East European regimes' five main radio services were monitored full time at RFE by a small platoon of men and women seldom seen and little known. Their job was to mine whatever nuggets of news or comment the communist regimes' airwaves carried. They then passed these on to translators who prepared the daily Monitoring Bulletin in English, inevitably a valuable if turgid feature of the total News Room budget. Occasionally, though, a nugget was unearthed that was truly priceless. Top-level communist purges were a case in point. But my favorite was when Radio Sofia carried a letter from Todor Zhivkov, president of Bulgaria, to the president of the Bulgarian Writers' Union giving him tips on topics the Union writers might cover in their next novels. Poor Zhivkov! He really was meaning to be helpful.

Field Offices and Bureaus

The RFE Field Bureaus fed Central News from afar. In the early days they were called plain Field Offices, and their main purpose was interviewing refugees from virtually anywhere in Eastern Europe, usually after they had passed through the various asylum processes. In Austria, for example, there were Field Offices in Vienna, Graz, Linz, and Salzburg; in Scandinavia, in Malmö and Stockholm; in Germany, Nuremberg, West Berlin, Frankfurt, and Munich.

They were "spy centers," said RFE's critics, East and West. Not quite true, but not far off: they were "information-gathering points." RFE interviewers were attached to the Field Offices, which were usually headed by an American with a wartime intelligence background. These interviewers met with "suitable" refugees, wrote reports, and presented them to their American office chief, who then relayed them to RFE in Munich. In Munich these "field reports" would then go, not to the News Department, but to Research, which "evaluated" them. (The Research Department began life as the Research *and Evaluation* Section).

Obviously, intelligence was "the name of the game." While still at the Field Office all reports would be given the standard front-page "layout," or format: brief summary in English, location of interview, source description, source reliability. Then would follow the report, sometimes in the language of source and sometimes in German. If considered of special interest an English translation would be made in Munich. Finally, the head of the Research section concerned, or his deputy, would make an evaluation. Then copies would be distributed to the RFE policy director and the research director, and a few copies would be sent to the appropriate Broadcast Service.

The whole operation became more and more a waste of time. It smacked of intelligence gathering of the crudest sort. When the practice was discontinued in the early 1970s, Jan Nowak objected strongly, pleading that a pearl was sometimes caught in the net. But his objections, though strong, never evolved into a typical "Nowak campaign." Abolitionists like myself knew we had won.

The Field Offices were then drastically reduced in number, and those that survived became regular journalistic bureaus, staffed by real correspondents. Ironically, though, the most famous ever RFE correspondent dated back to the old Field Office era. He was the legendary G. E. R. Gedye, the Briton who covered Vienna for several English newspapers during the 1930s and was the author of *Fallen Bastions*, a famous history of the betrayal and fall of Australian socialism in the 1930s. Gedye was long past his best when he got to RFE's Vienna office. He only came because it was a means of staying just that little bit longer in the city he loved. I met him once and was intrigued by his accent, pipe, brogues, tweeds, and end-of-nose spectacles, above all by the aura he exuded. He was well liked by a small diverse staff, ever ready to climb that extra Viennese staircase for him.

Back in Munich modern journalism was quickly catching up with the News Department. RFE in the early sixties hired Gene P. Mater, from the *New World Telegram and Sun* as its director. Mater insisted on a professional newsroom, and he got it. He was followed by Nat Kingsley, late of the *New York Herald Tribune*, experienced, amiable, broad of mind, and tolerant. Kingsley was director of news when the always-efficient Englishman, Jim Edwards, was RFE's correspondent in Paris. Edwards soon became a great admirer of General de Gaulle. His adulation permeated many of the reports he filed to Munich, infuriating some of the Americans but rather tickling "irreverentials" like myself. Edwards sometimes stretched Kingsley's sense of humor to the limit. But he was never openly censored, perhaps just spiked now and again. In another sign of RFE tolerance, Edwards later became director of news itself, a good one, the "professional's professional," as he was determined to be. He did, though, like several of his colleagues, sometimes wear his professionalism on his sleeve. He had succeeded Anatole Shub, a famous correspondent from the *Washington Post*.

RFE's News Department certainly had its share of famous names. But the work that made it truly famous was done by the unnamed ones: professionals and personalities, day in and day out, putting out a product never bettered anywhere.

Research

Research at Radio Free Europe began in serfdom. It was originally there solely to serve the Broadcast Services, doing what it was told and when it was told. It meekly accepted its lowly status in the feudal hierarchy.

Its servitude worked as follows: a Broadcast Service editor would get an idea for a program, summon a researcher from the appropriate research section, and requisition the necessary facts and figures, usually setting a time limit for delivery. The researcher would find and then deliver what was required. Sometimes the Broadcast Service editor would consult the researcher, not on his idea for a program but on fact and source reliability. Some Broadcast

Service editors saw Research's most important task as preparing the Daily Press Digests. This was a selection of what were judged the most informative articles in the East European communist press. For the Poles it involved about six hours a day of constant typing by four elderly researchers. Later photocopying (Xeroxing) was introduced, easing the typing burden immeasurably. Several broadcast editors subsequently complained that reading the photocopies was weakening their eyes.

The emancipation of Research began with Professor Dinko Tomašić, a Croatian-American scholar. He was a controversial figure because of his sociological theories, which the entire Serb nation considered libelous. But Tomašić's true place in intellectual history was his discovery in early 1959 of the scholarly potential of RFE's archives. He began pestering his superiors for money and manpower to get these archives organized and then exploited in the form of research papers on various aspects of communist governance in Eastern Europe.

Tomašić was inexplicably fired for his exertions after less than a year. But it had obviously been decided anyway that, because of Hungary in 1956, more prestige and resources should be given to both research and analysis. A new Research and Analysis Department was set up and several new, mostly American, analysts were hired to cover the different East European countries. As already mentioned, I was made responsible for Bulgaria and Romania.

The two most interesting appointments were those of George Urban as analyst for Hungary and Paul Collins as assistant director of the new department. Hungarian-born and recently with the BBC, Urban was obviously brilliant and proceeded to write a number of RFE background papers proving it. Never much of a team player, Urban was nevertheless a real addition. He left the Radio after a couple of years, later to return on a rather higher level.

Paul Collins was a dominating personality. He was a liberal Texan, a breed no longer extant. He was also from a Southern Baptist family (his father a minister) and was an alumnus of Baylor University. Paul's loyalty to his family's religious injunctions was clearly an inverted one: he discarded them all. He was loud, high, wide, and handsome, very considerate with his staff but also an unashamed go-getter. He was born with a generous helping of native wit on which he sometimes depended rather too heavily. A little deeper reading would not have hurt. He later became director of Research but left the Radio in the late sixties on realizing that further advancement was being resolutely blocked.

Building and Expanding

The East European members of Research and Analysis worked in the nationality Research Sections—from about ten in the Polish down to six in the Bulgarian. (The full Research complement was over sixty.) The entire RFE archives were based in those five sections. There was also a well-stocked, well-run RFE library. The Research Sections regularly received the *entire* East European communist daily and weekly press, metropolitan and provincial, and the specialist economic and cultural press. They also received copies of the main Western newspapers. The entire press was then carefully sifted and relevant information was transferred to "subject files" or "personal card indexes." Partial computerization in RFE came first to the News Department in the 1980s. It penetrated Research only slowly. Still I remember being astonished by the speed of retrieval even in the undeveloped sixties.

The East European researchers felt threatened by the new Anglo-American arrivals after 1956 and the policy behind their appointment. The new arrivals were paid better, had better working conditions, and were considered senior. But it was not just that; the East Europeans felt their self-esteem bruised. The standards of education in some schools and universities in precommunist Eastern Europe were very high, and many of RFE's researchers had been through them. Had communism not intervened, they would have risen to considerable professional heights. Now they were working in a Munich basement being "lorded" over by young and often naïve Americans. They were often unfair to their young American colleagues, but the young Americans often showed a lack of consideration for them. Those who did show them some regard were often surprised at the sympathetic response that was returned.

Research at RFE got its real boost from R. V. ("Dick") Burks, previously mentioned. Burks had held an academic post at Wayne

State University in Detroit to which he returned after his period at RFE. He was both an operator and a scholar and later moved up in the Radio from research director to policy director. Burks was thus well placed to strengthen the role of research both inside and outside the Radio.

Inside the Radio he helped to refine the departmental routine of preparing country "Situation Reports" and general "Background Reports." Situation Reports, one for each country, were issued at least once a week. They contained analyses of the main four or five developments in the country concerned. They were prepared in the five East European sections and edited by the responsible American country analysts. (Burks later hired two economic analysts). Background Reports were written by both the country analysts and the East European researchers, sometimes in combination. They were on broader subjects and usually written at some length. On "breaking" subjects requiring speedy analysis (say a Politburo purge in Czechoslovakia), either an East European researcher or a country analyst would write a brief paper for the News Room Budget. These were immediately useful for broadcasting.

Inside the building Dick Burks vigorously pressed the Broadcast Services to make greater use of the Research Department's output. He believed strongly that good analysis made good policy and that RFE's broadcasting should be imbued with what the Research and Analysis Department had to offer. Many broadcasters took some convincing. It necessitated changes of habit and attitudes, as well as a degree of unaccustomed humility. But eventually it worked—mostly.

Burks also knew many scholars on Eastern Europe, especially in the United States. Some scholars were already familiar with the RFE research products, but Burks patiently interested more. The department's fame certainly spread. Many scholars and journalists dropped in at RFE on visits to and from Eastern Europe. Many journalists cheerfully borrowed from RFE research papers without so much as a thought of judgment. But occasionally an article would appear in the American or West European press, highly positive on Radio Free Europe and its research. These contacts were particularly valuable during the long Fulbright hearings in Washington at the turn of the seventies.

Up the Ladder

In 1968–69 I went for a year to Columbia University as a fellow at the Research Institute on Communist Affairs, headed by Zbigniew Brzezinski (I had been preceded there by Kevin Devlin and Michael Gamarnikow). While at Columbia I was offered the directorship of RFE Research and Analysis, to be taken up on my return. Such senior posts had always been exclusively filled by U.S. citizens. I held dual British and U.S. citizenship, having been born in the United States of British immigrants. My father had died in New York when I was four and my mother immediately took the family back to England. Later I voted in British elections and served in the Royal Air Force. An American Supreme Court decision in 1966 reversed a previous U.S. law that had withdrawn the right of citizenship for such activities. I then "reclaimed" U.S. citizenship and duly became a holder of dual British-American nationality.

RFE at first wanted me to renounce my British citizenship in view of the Research offer, but I refused. They then repeated their offer without conditions, and I accepted it. I remained very grateful to the Radio for this accommodating generosity. Only in America, I think, would such be found. Later I became RFE deputy director and then director, still on two passports, still loyal to both countries, still loyal to what both countries stood for.

Countering Provincialism

One of the great problems the entire Radio always faced was the regional "provincialism" of most its East European staff. They were passionately interested in their own countries, but, true to tradition, their interest in their neighboring East European countries was minimal and often inimical. Their interest in Western Europe, and increasingly in the United States, was incomparably greater. It was part of Research's job to moderate that regional provincialism by writing "cross-reporting" papers on developments in one country pertinent enough for several Broadcast Services to use them, or on topics themselves of overall Eastern European interest—Comecon, for example, the Warsaw Pact, changes in Soviet policy toward Eastern Europe as a whole, or on social problems, like abortion. It was often hard work, but it slowly paid off. The sight of a Polish

Broadcast Service editor hurrying to Research's main office to get a just-published paper on, say, Romania, made all the patience seem worthwhile.

As Research's fame increased, so did the volume of outside subscriptions for its papers from academics, journalists, and Western governments. Some very big names appeared on that list: Hugh Seton-Watson in Britain, Richard Löwenthal in Western Germany, Pierre Hassner in France, Zbigniew Brzezinski in the United States, Viktor Meier in Switzerland, Paul Lendvai in Austria. These were just a few of the best known. Some of the most gratifying names, though, were those of unknown young students, mainly in the United States. A number of these later became famous and were not slow to thank RFE Research for its services.

Invigorating Youth

Some of my best hours were spent with the young American analysts. Generally they mixed well together and worked well together. Some went on to good careers in the U.S. government service. Happily, one or two were just too individualistic for any government. They were their own men. One of these disappeared without trace on the Left Bank in Paris. Another became editor of the Metropolitan Opera house journal in New York. A third became a distinguished foreign correspondent. A fourth made a fortune out of "soft porn."

At the risk of seeming invidious, I will single out just two of these younger colleagues. Fritz Ermarth was one of RFE's analysts on the Soviet Union and its relations with Eastern Europe. He was outstanding and later held important jobs in both the National Security Council and the CIA. Collegial and convivial, Ermarth was on the right of the political spectrum, very much so compared with some of his colleagues. He carried what he referred to as his "burden" lightly. His favorite story was of meeting a new young country analyst at RFE for the first time. Ermarth told the newcomer that he was a hawk on Vietnam; the newcomer said he was too. This response staggered Ermarth. It felt, he said, as if the stout rail of expectancy on which he had habitually leaned since joining RFE had suddenly snapped, leaving him in a wasteland of political disorientation.

Ross Johnson came to RFE Research from Stanford, Fletcher, and Columbia with an awesome analytical reputation. He fully lived up to it and also turned out to be an excellent colleague, quiet, private, and loyal. He later had a distinguished career at RAND in Santa Monica, was director of RFE in the late eighties, then the first director of the combined RFE/RL Research Institute, and later a fellow of the Hoover Institution at Stanford. I had occasion to be personally grateful to Ross Johnson on more than one occasion.

Another of the young American analysts deserves a paragraph to himself. This is because he was arrested as an American spy in Czechoslovakia shortly after the Soviet invasion in August 1968. Bright and popular, if a little wacky at times, Fred Eidlin had been an analyst for Czechoslovakia in Research for something less than two years before the Soviet invasion. He left RFE soon after the invasion, during those few months when it seemed that the Soviets were now not quite sure what to do with Czechoslovakia, just how repressive they should be. It was then that Eidlin, now having left RFE and no longer subject to the Radio's restrictions on travel in Eastern Europe, decided to visit the country he had been studying for so long. In his guileless way, he seemed to think that the Soviet invasion had been little more than a Warsaw Pact mobility exercise, leaving things more or less as they had been. He was arrested as he got off the plane at Prague airport, then charged with espionage. Eidlin conducted himself with dignity in court but was of course found guilty and then sentenced to six years' imprisonment. He was thoroughly shaken by the whole experience. But he was released after a few months following backstairs negotiations in which RFE's staunch enemy, Senator William Fulbright, was believed to have played an important part on Eidlin's behalf. Eidlin subsequently went off teaching somewhere in Canada. He was always remembered by me and his other colleagues with much affection.

But no one was closer to me than Bob Hutchings, whom I appointed my deputy when I became RFE director in 1978. It was an inspired choice on my part, so much so that I often thought our roles should have been reversed: he as director, me as his deputy. (He often thought so too.) Hutchings later became assistant for Eastern Europe at the National Security Council at the end of the

Cold War in 1989. He wrote a fine book about his experiences and subsequently became assistant dean of students at Princeton. Ermarth, Johnson, and Hutchings were just three out of an outstanding group of young men who served Radio Free Europe and helped keep me young.

There were, I'm afraid, no young women in the group. We were not yet mature enough for that. But though we did not hire any woman analysts, one simply grew up in our very midst. Anneli Ute Gabanyi, a German from Romania, joined the Romanian section of the RFE Research and Analysis Department in 1969. At first she analyzed cultural developments in Romania but later moved into broader Romanian political developments. It soon became obvious that she was brilliant. She left RFE in 1987 and eventually joined the Stiftung Wissenschaft und Politik in Berlin.

In the year 2000 I wrote this about her: "Anneli Ute Gabanyi was an analyst in Radio Free Europe's Research and Analysis Department at a time when several brilliant analysts were enhancing the Department's and their own international reputations. Among them she was second to none. Anneli also figured prominently on German television during the fall of Ceaușescu and later Romanian developments. She was not just an analyst, she was a star."

7

Nationalism, Anti-Semitism, and Common Sense

Radio Free Europe never broadcast to Yugoslavia.[4] It was lucky it didn't. There was too much history around it. True, some of the most murderous eruptions of ethnic violence there occurred after 1989, after communism collapsed. But the ghastly memories of the Yugoslav ethnic massacres during World War II, just a few years before RFE was established, were still fresh. And they were more than fresh in the long memories of those Yugoslav exiles in the West from among whom any RFE Yugoslav service would have been recruited. Any such Yugoslav service would have destroyed itself in just a few months and would have taken the whole of Radio Free Europe with it. The Stalin-Tito break, the ostensible reason for abandoning the idea of Yugoslav broadcasting, not only began the erosion of world communism but also saved RFE from an early grave.

RFE thus ducked Yugoslavia's nationalisms. But it could not duck Eastern Europe's. What it could do, though, and its survival depended on it, was to keep nationalism off the air. This it did. It was one of Radio Free Europe's greatest achievements, made possible by the management's wisdom and firmness and by the East European staff's realism and restraint. What follows, therefore, is not a rundown on what RFE broadcast but on what it did not broadcast.

Take Polish nationalism first. This was essentially defensive during the RFE years, and it centered on the Oder-Neisse (Odra-Nysa) Line. The Oder-Neisse was Poland's new western frontier (officially only *pro tem*), drawn by the allies at the end of World War II to compensate Poland for the loss of large eastern territories to the Soviet Union. Poland, therefore, marched one step west at the expense of prewar Germany. There was strong opposition in the new Federal Republic of Germany (West Germany) to the permanent recognition of this frontier, mainly from the Christian Democrats (CDU), the Christian Social Union in Bavaria (the CDU's sister party), and elements of the West German press. There was clearly opposition, too, from influential officials in the German Foreign Office. The most vociferous opponents of all were the West German expellee organizations representing the millions of Germans who fled or were expelled from Poland at the end of the war. (See chapter 2.)

The expellees regarded the RFE Poles as their enemies, Jan Nowak especially. Every Pole in fact, in exile or at home, regarded the sanctity of the Oder-Neisse Line as essential for Poland's future. Nowak's immediate problem, though, was not the formidable German opposition to permanent recognition of the Oder-Neisse (he expected that), but the refusal by RFE's American management, obviously influenced by State Department hesitations, to allow the Polish Service to broadcast its support for the Oder-Neisse. Nowak knew that this was seriously hurting RFE in Poland and playing into the hands of regime propaganda claiming that its silence showed that, despite its pretensions, RFE was nothing but a tool of "German revanchism."

Nowak tackled the problem his way. In 1958 he informed the RFE management that the Polish Service would stop work unless allowed to express support for the Oder-Neisse Line. Just before the strike was due to begin he got his way. Washington's line softened. It was a great moral and political victory for RFE's Poles. Later, of course, with Willy Brandt's *Ostpolitik* and the full German recognition of the Oder-Neisse, this victory was confirmed. It was also another milestone in the honorable record of RFE's Polish Service. First, the Światło coup, then its record over the "Polish October," now the Oder-Neisse victory, all in considerably less than ten years.

Slovak Separatism

Most RFE exiles were united in their nationalism. But the Czechoslovak Service was divided by nationalism. It was always on the defensive against West German "revanchism," especially over the Sudeten issue, but it was Slovak nationalism that threatened its unity the most deeply, a precursor to the issue that eventually led to the breakup of Czechoslovakia itself.

RFE's Slovak editors were overwhelmingly Protestant or Jewish. Roman Catholics, who comprised about 90 percent of the population of Slovakia, were represented for many years on the Broadcast Service by one Catholic editor. He was Jozef Šramek, a gregarious soul, staunch in his religion, and the object of considerable interest on account of the lonely furrow he was plowing.

One of my most pleasant duties later as director of Radio Free Europe was to visit Rome occasionally to keep our bridges with the Vatican in good repair. After all, by far most of our listeners were Roman Catholic. The Polish connection was obviously the most important. Over the years, especially with Karol Wojtyła on the throne of St. Peter, I met an impressive array of Polish clergy in Rome. But on one occasion Šramek chaperoned my visit. Under his aegis I met several elderly Slovak Monsignori as well as the top Slovak cleric in Rome, Archbishop Jozef Tomko, a favorite of John Paul II who was later elevated to cardinal. Behind their unfailing courtesy, it was obvious that every Slovak cleric I met was an anti-Czech nationalist and had little time for Radio Free Europe. There was, in fact, a strong whiff of clerical fascism about them. One of them told me how much he had admired Father Tiso.

To be fair to RFE's Slovaks, during the Radio's short history they had to put up with much Czech arrogance and deliberate demonstrations of Czech superiority. An early Czechoslovak Broadcast Service director had had to be dismissed because of his open contempt for Slovaks. Some Czechs, for their part, complained about Slovak ultrasensitivity, and even some Slovaks admitted to this. But eventually the most encouraging thing about the Slovak psychology was that most young Slovaks soon lost their inferiority complex *vis à vis* the Czechs. In the prewar first republic Czechs had to do almost everything in Slovakia, simply because the Slovaks were too backward. This humiliated and angered educated Slovaks,

especially the younger ones. But by the 1980s Czechs were no longer necessary; the Slovaks could do things for themselves. This was
the key transformation in the Czech-Slovak relationship. It made it
even more difficult, but much healthier.

Hungarian Irredentism

"Nem, Nem Soha!" I never heard it myself in RFE, but among some
senior Hungarians there its spirit was pervasive. "No, No Never"—
it was the rallying cry of Hungarian irredentists, practically the
whole nation, in the interwar period. They were refusing to accept
the massive territorial losses Hungary suffered through the Treaty
of Trianon after the end of World War I.

There had even been some pious hopes after World War II that
at least some of the lost territories might still be recovered. István
Bede had been one of Budapest's top diplomats sent to the West
(Bede to London) to try to persuade the victorious allies to soften
the Trianon blow. This mini offensive had no chance. Bede, for his
part, had the breadth and the brains to see that Old Hungary was
no more. He never betrayed any interest in the matter while at RFE.

Others, though, did. The radio canteen was a favorite haunt for
irredentism. So were the private homes of many RFE Hungarians.
And with the irredentism went contempt for Slovaks and Romanians,
the nations Hungarians had once suppressed. (Irredentists were
usually anti-Semitic, too, though many Hungarian Jews were also
irredentist.)

But the unavoidable generational change that occurred at the
Radio in the 1960s led to a marked lowering of the nationalist
temperature among RFE's exiles. The younger Hungarians,
especially, had broader interests and sympathies. They were more
"Western" (despite, or because of, their years behind the Iron
Curtain), and had more sympathy with Hungary's former subject
nations. Some of them were suspect to their older colleagues
precisely because of their breadth of mind. József Szabados, Bede's
successor, typified that younger generation. He understood his
compatriots' irredentism and despised it.

But all RFE's Hungarians, old and young, irredentists and
realists, were resentful of the growing discrimination against the

Hungarian minorities in both Transylvania and Slovakia. This discrimination had been a strong feature of the reemergence of Romanian nationalism in the late fifties and of Slovak nationalism in the sixties.

RFE's Hungarians knew that some Hungarians at home and in the communist Hungarian regime itself strongly resented the worsening condition of the Hungarian minorities. Many Hungarian intellectuals in Hungary, both pro- and anti-regime, refused to keep silent about it. The pressure was such that there had to be a big crack soon in the official silence in Budapest.

It came in an article in 1971 by the influential Politburo member Zoltan Komoscin. His reference to the minority in Transylvania was oblique but unmistakable. It virtually coincided with Ceauşescu's return from a visit to China and North Korea, a visit that had infuriated the Soviet Union, and its timing led to much speculation about Moscow supporting Hungary on the minority issue. RFE's Hungarian Service reported fully on Komoscin's article, the furious Romanian response to it, and the ensuing international press comment and speculation. But the service wisely made no direct comment of its own.

Romanian Responses

The international commotion over Transylvania led to a defensiveness on the part of most Romanians, nowhere more so than among those in Radio Free Europe. Nor was anyone more aware than they (although they would never admit it) of the dubious reputation their nation had historically labored under throughout the whole of Europe. But at RFE they felt an almost siege-like mentality, especially *vis à vis* the Hungarians. Though there were more than twice as many Romanians in Romania as Hungarians in Hungary, it was exactly the reverse in RFE. And the Hungarian Service broadcast more than twice as many hours as the Romanian. The Hungarian emigration, too, was much larger and stronger than the Romanian. Perhaps most hurting of all was that Hungarian culture was Central European. Romania's culture, though derivatively streaked with the French, was Byzantine-Balkan. Its religion was Orthodox, whereas Hungary's was Roman Catholic and Protestant, that is, West European.

I myself bumped up against Romanian sensitivity in 1964 when I wrote an article for the West German monthly *Der Monat* on Romania's budding independence policy. I made the immature error of quoting, albeit with abundant caveats, a German general in World War I who described the Romanians as the "whores of Europe" on account of their apparently compulsive habit of changing allies. This brought down the wrath of my Romanian colleagues on my unsuspecting head. But my cardinal sin, as one of them told me, was that one Romanian colleague had seen two Hungarians reading *Der Monat* in the corridor and "laughing over it." He had no doubt it was my offending article that was causing their mirth. But forgiving comes easily to Romanians, and we all soon got over it.

Bulgarian Sadness

The Bulgarians are a sad people. History has made them losers—in 1014 when the Great Bulgarian Empire fell, virtually its entire army blinded by the Byzantines; in 1878 when, after 500 years of Ottoman rule, the Bulgarians had their hopes of a large independent state dashed; then in 1912–13, frustrated by a catastrophic defeat in the second Balkan War; finally in the two World Wars when they backed Germany both times in the hope of recovering Macedonia.

The Bulgarians hardly deserved their misfortune. And virtually the whole Bulgarian population stuck to its conviction that Macedonians were ethnically Bulgarian and that the so-called "Macedonian language" was rightfully Bulgarian, dressed up by a few opportunists in Skopje to make it look original. Very few Bulgarians, even today, remain immune to the bitterness of history. Their obvious symptom is an inferiority complex. The Bulgarians at RFE had one, collectively and singly.

The RFE environment hardly helped. They were the smallest group there and broadcast the least number of hours, between seven and eight per day. This was discouraging enough, but most discouraging of all was the fact that nothing ever seemed to be happening in Bulgaria. The glib explanation for this was that Bulgarians were pro-Russian and took kindly to communism anyway. Though the latter is quite untrue, there is truth in the former: the historical and cultural links with the Russians were strong. But many Bulgarians strongly resented the way the Russians took them for granted. They always insisted that their own identity be preserved and nourished. Actually, several RFE Bulgarians were from that rising economic class that had been primarily pro-German. Certainly most of RFE's older Bulgarians denied that they had ever been pro-Russian, while the younger generation genuinely resented the inferior status to which the Bulgarian communist regime, with its relentless adulation of all things Soviet, had bent their compatriots.

But all RFE's Bulgarians, like their compatriots at home, were united on Macedonia. Some, again mostly young, were prepared to admit that the Bulgarian occupation, under Hitler's auspices, of part of Macedonia in World War II had been inept and had tarnished Bulgaria's noble record on anti-Semitism. But on the *principle* of the matter there was no generational division. RFE was lucky that there was nobody in the building to argue with them. But had it broadcast to Yugoslavia too....!

The Bulgarian Broadcast Service faithfully observed RFE's rules on reporting territorial and ethnic questions. They were loyal and capable colleagues. Even when incensed over the way the Macedonian government in Yugoslavia and its media distorted history and "stole" historical Bulgarian heroes, they dutifully confined themselves to reporting the growing robust ripostes of the Sofia media. They were pleased whenever Moscow followed up a phase of bad relations with Belgrade by allowing Sofia more leeway to air its case about Macedonia. And they were doubly pleased when the Bulgarian regime eventually plucked up courage on Macedonia by broadcasting material obviously without waiting for Soviet permission. "Surrogate nationalism," this came to be called, although RFE's Bulgarians shuddered at the word "surrogate."

Anti-Semitism

It was there all right. Forbidden in the programs, it remained embedded in the culture of most East Europeans. Some of the RFE staff wrestled with it in their own consciences, with varying degrees of success. Obviously the Holocaust and its exposures had done much to persuade them that anti-Semitism was unacceptable. But, still, some retained what they regarded as their "mild" anti-Semitism.

Some Romanians were uneasy about their boss, Noel Bernard, who was of Jewish origin, not being "a real Romanian." There was one Pole, a self-conscious individualist, who trotted out banal anti-Semitic remarks "because that's what you people expect from us Poles." Sometimes, too, he would gleefully and correctly point out how strong anti-Semitism was in France historically, not to mention in Britain and the United States. Yet he was the kind of man who would have stoutly defended any Jew who needed it.

Radio Free Europe never faced the "Jewish problem" to the extent that Radio Liberty did. As dissidence increased in the Soviet Union in the seventies, RL launched a big drive to recruit Jewish refugees. This inevitably led to friction. Actually RFE was sometimes criticized for hiring "too few Jews," taking a "token few" but very few more. To some extent it deserved this criticism. But not many Jews were now available, and few of them fancied working in Germany anyway. It is worth remembering, too, that two of the Radio's most prominent Broadcast Service directors, Julius Firt (Czechoslovak) and Bernard (Romanian) were Jewish, as was the Polish Service's star economics editor, Michael Gamarnikow. At least four Czechoslovak editors, three Polish, and three Hungarians were Jewish. So was Hanus Hajek, longtime brilliant head of Czechoslovak Research.

A strongly sensitive reaction among many of RFE's East Europeans occurred when one's nation was charged with anti-Semitism. The equanimity of several of my Polish friends at the Radio was visibly disturbed on such occasions. Jan Nowak usually became Vesuvian over them. When I talked to David Halberstam in the late sixties about Poland, he talked about anti-Semitism there. When I asked how it still manifested itself, especially with so few Jews left, he replied, "By bloody silly remarks." "Only the Jews get telephones" was an example he gave. I tactlessly told Nowak about this. He exploded and from then on expunged Halberstam from his list of "serious people." But Halberstam was promptly restored to that crucial list when he gave RFE a much-needed boost at the Fulbright Senate hearings.

The Trifa Episode

No discussion of anti-Semitism, actual or alleged, at RFE would be complete without a few lines on the "Trifa episode." It was a case of RFE's being accused of anti-Semitism rather than being guilty of it. All the same, it cast little credit on a number of its staff, including myself.

On 1 May 1979 RFE's Romanian Service broadcast an interview between Liviu Floda, its "stringer" in New York, and Bishop Valerian ("Viorel") Trifa, the head of the Romanian Orthodox Church in America. Trifa, as a priest in World War II, had soiled the reputation of the Romanian Orthodox Church and of humanity generally by ferociously encouraging an Iron Guard frenzy against Jews in Bucharest. After the war he had crept into the United States and quietly resumed serving his Church there. The occasion for the interview was an important anniversary of the Romanian Orthodox Church's foundation in the United States. Noel Bernard, who had ordered the interview, thought the anniversary should be marked and was eager to upstage a splinter Romanian Orthodox Church in the States that was under communist control.

I saw the announcement of the interview in the notice of Romanian programs for that day and immediately warned Bernard about it. I later heard that several of his own editors had done the same. Floda himself had also objected. I knew enough about Trifa to suspect he could mean trouble. Bernard assured me that the proposed interview was "harmless." When the interview was broadcast, I was soon reminded of the trouble I had feared by a letter from a Dr. Stone, a dentist in New York, complaining bitterly about the Trifa interview and about the whole ethos of a Radio that would even talk to such a man. Dr. Stone had apparently been tipped off by two Romanian Service editors in Munich. The actual content of the interview was indeed quite harmless. But that was hardly the point.

One point of interest was that all the protagonists in this case were Jewish: Bernard, Floda, Dr. Stone, and his RFE informants. But then Congresswoman Elizabeth Holtzman (herself Jewish) was tipped off about the story. Mrs. Holtzman, a prominent New York Democrat, was conducting a vigorous campaign at the time against Nazi war criminals in the United States. She proceeded to organize a meeting of a subcommittee of the House Committee on Foreign Affairs during which, well supplied with material from Bernard's enemies in Munich, she denounced him as unsuitable for the post he held.

The matter was also taken up by a meeting in Washington of the Board for International Broadcasting. Not surprisingly (and not undeservedly), RFE Munich took a drubbing. Neither was Munich's cause helped by Paul Henze, Bill Griffith's old deputy in the 1950s in RFE Policy, a long-serving CIA operative now working under Zbigniew Brzezinski at the National Security Council. Henze showed a remarkable lack of political sensitivity when he tried to defend, or explain, the Trifa interview. He only kept the pot boiling.

All in all, a very bad episode for RFE. Everybody came out of it badly. Its worst aspect was that it tagged the Radio with a suspicion of anti-Semitism that it did not deserve.

One other aspect of the Trifa episode is worth mentioning. It was broadcast not from Munich but from New York. Had it been scheduled as a Munich program, I would have overruled Bernard and killed it. The truth was that nobody in Munich cared much about New York programming. RFE's programming—and I was enthusiastic about this—had become almost exclusively European. We left programming about the United States almost entirely to the Voice of America (VOA). And yet some of our few New York programs, especially Karl Reyman's weekly comments about American politics, were outstanding, certainly better than anything VOA carried. The trouble was that the drift towards *European* programming, begun after 1956, had continued unchecked. The Radio was called to account for this when the Reagan sea change took place (see chapter 10). Up to a point, we deserved it.

8

Communism in Nonstop Decay

One thing is clear from my memorandum quoted in chapter 5: I was not expecting communism in Eastern Europe to end as soon as it did. I was even planning for its future! What I didn't realize was the impending collapse of the Soviet Union. It certainly wasn't obvious at the time. The common belief remained that the Soviet Union was strong enough to hold what it had and to set the ultimate parameters for Eastern Europe.

Communist rule in Eastern Europe in the early seventies was seen by some observers as having emerged strengthened from its 1968 ordeal. The Soviets had reaffirmed their strength and determination. Czechoslovakia was "pacified." "Flash-point" Poland, after the shock of Gomułka's fall in 1970, was seen as recovering its strength and stability under its new leader, Edward Gierek. Hungary was prospering under Kádár, who knew his limits of movement and maneuver. Bulgaria was as always. And even Romania, though boldly criticizing the invasion of Czechoslovakia, had presumably been sufficiently chastened by it.

Many observers also saw Western policy as serving to strengthen the communist grip on Eastern Europe. Détente, they averred, was doing just that. The extensive Western financial loans to most East European regimes were heavily criticized for allegedly building up the communist economies and strengthening them.

Mixed Views on Helsinki

The opposition to détente reached a new intensity with "Helsinki," the Conference on Security and Co-operation in Europe (CSCE) held in Helsinki in 1975. For some this was Moscow's icing on the cake, a triumphant monument to Soviet diplomacy and depressing proof of Western gullibility. (CSCE later became OSCE—O for Organization).

I myself shared this skepticism about Helsinki at the time and for several years afterwards. I had generally approved of détente, especially of the German *Ostpolitik*, in spite of the dangers it held for Radio Free Europe's survival in Munich. But Helsinki was a treaty too far.

In my book, *Eastern Europe and Communist Rule* (Duke University Press, 1988), I wrote that "Helsinki was indeed an act of cynicism and was regarded as such by the populations of the countries concerned." The follow-up meetings after Helsinki—Belgrade, Madrid, Vienna, Stockholm, Bern, Budapest, and so on—I described as "boring charades, divorced from the realities of the situation, scrambling after a meaningful consensus." Strong words shared by many, not least at Radio Free Europe.

Looking back on Helsinki later, I realized how wrong I had been. It became clear to me that the key issue was the *context* in which the agreement took place. That context covered the decline of communist self-belief, the communists' recognition of their own economic weaknesses, their basic fear of their own people, and the collapse of their ideology. In that *context* Helsinki and its follow-ups became another unnerving drip-drip-drip on communist morale. Having to publish in their own countries the full texts of the Helsinki Agreement, which they did, was an important ideological surrender. Many intellectuals in the region photocopied these full texts and distributed them. Had Eastern Europe been a sea of tranquility at the time, Helsinki would have made no difference. But it was far from tranquil, and Helsinki put another hole through a dike that was becoming ever more porous. Both intellectuals and workers began punching so many holes that the dike simply collapsed.

And in 1977, obviously against the background of Helsinki, "Charter 77" was published in Prague, the first exciting proof of the rebirth of the Czech intellectual tradition and an inspiring sign that the spirit of freedom was still alive in Prague. It was as a result of Charter 77 that RFE fully entered the "*Samizdat* business." Already throughout the 1970s underground literature, mainly from Poland, Czechoslovakia, and Hungary, had been reaching the West. What began as a trickle soon became a wave. Some of this literature was in book form, but most of it was in the form of papers written by intellectuals for a small domestic readership and with the specific aim of being smuggled to the West, mainly to Radio Free Europe. RFE would then select the items to be broadcast back. (*Samizdat* from the Soviet Union also came in bulk volume to Radio Liberty, where it received the same treatment). Subjects covered ranged from the iniquities of the communist system to environmental, literary, and philosophical issues. Charter 77 gave Czechoslovak *samizdat* a real boost.

Western Europe's Influence

The *context* in which the Helsinki Agreement was signed had begun to take shape several years before. The main lesson of the Soviet invasion of Czechoslovakia had been the barrenness of communist ideology. It killed any prospect of communist reform. This ideology, the core and sinews of communist strength, had declined immeasurably. From now on communist rule was a weird mixture of appeasing society and repressing it when necessary.

Intellectuals in Eastern Europe gradually began to realize this historic change. They began to note with approval the historic changes that had been taking place in Western Europe since the early 1960s. What interested both them and Radio Free Europe most about Western Europe was what eventually became the European Union (EU). Established by six countries through the Treaty of Rome in 1957 and beginning operations in 1958, the Common Market, as it was first called, was a perfectly legitimate propaganda weapon for the Radio, especially so because it almost immediately became the target for furious Soviet and East European official attacks. The gist of these attacks was that the Common Market was the creation of West European capitalists aimed at enriching themselves. Guiding and ultimately dominating it was the not-so-hidden hand of Wall Street. Compare this with their own Council for Mutual Economic Assistance (Comecon), the communist media urged, and you would see the difference between exploitation and disinterested cooperation.

This communist campaign against the Common Market prompted RFE Research to publish a booklet in 1966 entitled *The Communists and the Common Market*. It was among the first RFE Research publications to win international acclaim, and a German edition was soon published. In the meantime RFE's broadcast interest in the Common Market's economics and politics developed apace. A Radio bureau in Brussels was established to cover both it and the NATO alliance. As the Common Market progressed and evolved, it helped generate an astonishing economic prosperity among its members. It thus became an even more potent weapon in the Radio's arsenal, a weapon strengthened by the fact that more Poles and Hungarians were being allowed to travel to the West. They saw things for themselves, reported back on the economic transformation that was taking place, and gave the lie to communist claims that the West European masses were being pauperized.

Eurocommunism and Helsinki's Course

In the mid-1960s Radio Free Europe also began broadcasting news about the West European communist parties. As the communist world became fissured by the Tito-Stalin break, the Albanian defection, the Romanian deviation, and above all by the Sino-Soviet dispute, so several West European communist parties attracted attention by their own unwillingness to accept the "leading role" of the Soviet party. Thus "Euro-Communism" came into being.

It was the Italian party that drew most attention, first under Palmiro Togliatti and then more intensely under Enrico Berlinguer. RFE Research published many papers on its policy and writings, and the Broadcast Services used many of them. The intellectual quality of some of the Italian communists was outstanding. I personally was keen on RFE's broadcasting these signs of Italian single-minded determination, because I realized the interest in the subject among East European intellectuals. Others in the Radio did, too. We were encouraged to persist by having in Research Kevin Devlin, an Irishman formerly with the *Guardian*. Devlin became the world's greatest expert on the Western communist parties and was an excellent writer to boot. We were subsequently criticized in the West for "overdoing" the Western communist parties. Perhaps at times Enrico Berlinguer and his "Long March through the Institutions" did get more attention than they deserved. But we meant to stress, not to exaggerate, their importance. As Devlin himself said years later: "One sentence from Pope John Paul II is worth more to us than a whole issue of *Unità*."

Despite its early (and mistaken) reservations about CSCE, or "Helsinki," Radio Free Europe followed its process more zealously than any radio station or newspaper in either Europe or the United States. It sent correspondents not only to the conference at Helsinki itself but to all the follow-up conferences as well. Its first correspondent was Iain MacDonald, my own first RFE boss, whose analyses of the implications of CSCE were of a very high order. MacDonald died in 1976 and was replaced by Roland Eggleston, an Australian. Eggleston was the classic "legman" and became the best-known journalist throughout the entire Helsinki process. He was well known among its communist as well as its Western representatives. At his news conference at the end of one of the CSCE's Madrid sessions, the first words of Max Kampelman, the chief American delegate, were "Where's Roly? I can't begin without Roly."

Vietnam Coverage

The Vietnam War was a serious problem for RFE's management, partly because many intellectuals in our audience were opposed to it. Somewhere in an RFE mission statement or basic guidance, it was stated that RFE's foreign line should "not be inconsistent with the broad lines of American foreign policy." This was a masterly expression presumably designed to give the Radio a certain flexibility in its handling of world affairs. But Vietnam was *war*, not foreign policy, and it would have been understandable had the U.S. government of the day insisted on a rigorous pro-America line with regard to it. But apparently it did not; at least the Radio's American top management did not act as if it did.

Dick Burks was policy director during part of the war. He

obviously had no doubts about the justice of the American cause or about the inevitability of an American victory. He issued a few program guidances to this effect, with which the Broadcast Services dutifully complied. Generally, though, RFE's stand on the war was one of neutrality. Some of the younger Americans were spiritedly against it. The war was certainly not ignored in broadcasts, but the usual means of covering it came through the daily International Press Reviews carried by all the services, a feature program that excerpted or summarized the best European and American newspapers on the big issues of the day. Generally, though not exclusively, these reviews expressed editorial opinions against the war. RFE's coverage of the Vietnam War did much to keep its credibility among the intellectual and younger members of its audience. The contrast between Radio Free Europe's coverage and the Voice of America's was striking.

The Big Blows in Poland

The evolution of European unity, Eurocommunism, and what became known as the "Helsinki process" began the weakening, the "softening up," of communism in Eastern Europe. But these would be essentially long term in their effects. What was needed now was a knockout blow. And, not surprisingly, it came from Poland.

The hollowness of Poland's economic prosperity in the first few years of Gierek's rule became obvious in the breakdown of 1976 and the increases in food prices that were the regime's only answer to it. The Polish workers' answer to it was widespread strikes. It was indeed 1970 all over again, but with one significant difference. The striking workers were on their own in 1970; in 1976 they were joined by the intellectuals.

Many Poles had begun to despair of any renewal of the worker-intellectual cooperation that had been such a feature of the Polish October of 1956. But what aroused the intellectuals now were the extraordinary police brutality and the victimization of a large number of the striking workers. The Workers Defense Committee (KOR) was formed by a number of intellectuals. KOR began with about thirty intellectuals who made contact with many workers, and these two elements were soon reconciled. Two names at first stood out in KOR: Jacek Kuroń, once an idealistic communist now a superb publicist, and Adam Michnik, later editor of what became, and still is, Poland's top newspaper of note, *Gazeta Wyborcza*.

The ferment spawned other intellectual groups, too, most notably ROPCiO (Movement for the Defense of Human and Civil Rights). ROPCiO was more nationalistic than KOR, but most nationalist of all was the KPN (Confederation for an Independent Poland). Though relatively small, its nationalism carried real appeal. There was a noticeable anti-Semitic element in both the KPN and ROPCiO, as there was later in Solidarity, the dominating trade union movement.

RFE responded enthusiastically to the reemergence of worker-intellectual cooperation. It had noted its previous decline in silence. To have broadcast about it might well have been seen as interference or advice, something the listeners never wanted. Again, the main dictum of RFE policy since 1956 came into play: let events speak for themselves. The Radio's policy makers were worried about the signs of anti-Semitism. But these were small, certainly in relation to the momentous developments underway. The Polish Service was kept well informed by the increasing number of knowledgeable travelers coming from Poland. This, combined with the patient scrutiny of the Polish press and monitoring of Radio Warsaw, made the Polish Service better informed than any other Western organization, overt or covert.

The Pope and Solidarity

The revival of the worker-intellectual alliance in the face of police brutality against the strikers (itself a sign not of regime strength but of weakness) was the beginning of the communist collapse in Poland.

This collapse continued and culminated in two events that changed the entire course of history. The first was the election in October 1978 of Karol Cardinal Wojtiła, Archbishop of Kraków, as pope. The second was the establishment in Poland in 1980 of a *free* trade union, Solidarity. The first event dramatized and completed the rout of communism as an ideology; the second fatally weakened the entire structure of communism. A Soviet KGB officer who was in Warsaw during the pope's first visit the following summer later told a Western journalist, "I remember thinking, this is it, it's all over." And throughout the world many people must have been remembering Stalin's famous question, "How many divisions has the Pope?" The Polish people were giving him their answer.

John Paul II died in 2005 one day before this part of my book was being written. In a tribute to him in *The Guardian*, Timothy Garton Ash wrote:

> No one can prove conclusively that he was a primary cause of the end of communism. However, the major figures on all sides—not just Lech Wałęsa, the Polish Solidarity Leader, but also Solidarity's arch opponent, General Wojciech Jaruzelski; not just the former American president George Bush Senior but also the former Soviet president Mikhail Gorbachev— now agree that he was. I would argue the historical case in three steps: the Polish pope and the Solidarity revolution in Poland in 1980; without Solidarity, no dramatic change in Soviet policy towards Eastern Europe under Gorbachev; without that change, no velvet revolutions in 1989.

The papal election electrified the Poles at RFE. They had been buoyant enough since 1976 with the renewed worker-intellectual alliance. Now they felt that Poland's history, and their own, was really being transformed. (The award shortly afterward of the Nobel Prize for Literature to Czesław Miłosz, which normally would have been an occasion for the greatest jubilation, now simply had to take its place in the long line of momentous Polish achievements).

The first papal visit to Poland in 1979 was a tiring but gratifying experience for the Polish Service. One of its editors summed it up best with self-mocking rue in his concluding program on it: "They say the Pope has lost six pounds on his visit. Well, I have lost eight, and every ounce of it has been worth it." The RFE Research Department also exerted itself by publishing a booklet *The Pope in Poland*. It was mainly edited by Jan de Weydenthal, the department's Polish analyst at the time, and was widely published in North America and Western Europe.

The Polish Service now braced itself for the next almost

inevitable outbreak of labor unrest. This began in August 1980 and, as ten years earlier, was centered on Gdańsk, with a new Polish hero, Lech Wałęsa, as its leader. Now, more than ever, was the time for careful reporting and restrained comment. Then, as the year wore on, it seemed that something new and enthralling might be emerging. The regime was turning out even weaker than even the most blithe optimist had thought, and strikers were stronger and more politically coherent. Then the strikers' demand became clear: *a free trade union*. Never! At least that was my reaction, and I think it was generally shared. Then it came; the Polish regime surrendered and agreed. Our jubilation was touched with fearfulness. What would Moscow do? The Russians simply couldn't let it happen. But they seemed to. At least for now.

The Research Department again rose to the occasion by publishing a major-length book on the strikes, centered on the tense month of August 1980. It was simply called *August 1980: The Strikes in Poland* and was edited by William F. Robinson. It was probably the most important RFE publication. Like *The Pope in Poland*, it was widely read in the West.

It was a pity for Jan Nowak that he had retired in 1975, just before these huge triumphs. He went to live in the United States, just outside Washington. Before leaving Europe he had written a book of reminiscences of his wartime activity with the Polish underground, *Courier from Warsaw*. In Washington he vigorously pursued Polish causes and became a well-known, much-respected figure. He visited Poland several times after 1989 and returned to live there in 2002. He died in Warsaw in 2005 at the age of 90. They saw him off in style.

Nowak was replaced at RFE by Zygmunt Michałowski, Kraków-born and Kraków-cultured. Michałowski, an experienced broadcaster, had high intelligence, charm, and keen humor. He was reasonable and tolerant, perhaps too much so in view of the egos on the Polish Service. He lacked Nowak's dynamism and suffered from the eruptions of intrigue among the Polish diaspora. But he was a successful service director and did a superb job after the Papal election in 1978, and then during the tumultuous year of 1980. It must be added here that Michael Gamarnikow died of cancer in 1981. His contribution had also been immense.

Poland in 1981, after the free trade union triumph, was similar in some respects to Czechoslovakia in 1968, the basic difference being that in Czechoslovakia change came through the communist party; in Poland it came against it. Great reform breakthroughs were made in both countries. The key question now in Poland, as it had been in Czechoslovakia, was whether the reform momentum could be sufficiently slowed or moderated to appease Soviet concern. And the mystery regarding the possible Soviet response remained as deep as ever.

But in Poland, as in Czechoslovakia, what became obvious was that the momentum of reform could not be slowed. This had become evident, too, in Hungary in 1956. Thus, one of the great defining characteristics of the communist system in Eastern Europe was again confirmed—that once dissatisfaction with it had been allowed to develop, then its pace quickened, its comprehensiveness broadened, and its implications deepened. The very survival of the system was soon at stake, and the near certainty of armed Soviet intervention in Poland apparently loomed.

The crisis came to a head in 1981, and the one man who might possibly have controlled the impetus for change, Stefan Cardinal Wyszyński, died in May 1981. Nothing should obscure the tremendous work over thirty years that Cardinal Wyszyński did for Poland, first in resisting and then in beating back communist power. He was always at the very forefront of Polish politics. Had he not died at this crucial time, he might have helped calm an increasingly frantic situation. It must be remembered also that John Paul himself was the target of an assassination attempt that same month, May 1981. Had he not been disabled for a considerable period, and had Wyszyński lived, then these two extraordinary leaders might have helped avoid the eventual repression of Solidarity in December 1981 and the dashing (at least temporarily) of the great hopes invested in it.

The year 1981 was probably the most difficult in the entire history of the Polish Service at RFE. It naturally supported Solidarity but without seeking to stir the new free trade union to further conquests. In 1981 the attention of the world was on Poland, and there was almost too much intelligent Western press comment to use. The Polish Service used this comment as a means of showing its listeners that they were both making history and had a responsibility to history. The service skillfully blended world press comment about the dangers of Poland's geopolitical situation with reminders of the Soviet Union's record of interventions against its own allies. The great difficulty was in avoiding specific advice. RFE broadcasts were forbidden to do this anyway, but both Michałowski and I felt strongly that well-fed, well-paid, well-housed exiles enjoying the safety and security of living in the West were never in any position to proffer advice to listeners living in the hardships and dangers of Eastern Europe. Michałowski and I used to meet most mornings, and I was continually impressed by his wisdom.

Cardinal Wyszyński's death and the pope's near-death at the hands of an assassin were given much coverage not only by the Polish Service but also by all RFE's Broadcast Services. Every service paid tribute to Wyszyński as a great man. As for the assassination attempt on the pope, the services were instructed not to jump to conclusions about who or what was behind the gunman in St Peter's Square.

After a man like Wyszyński any new Primate was almost bound to be a disappointment. But his successor, Józef Cardinal Glemp, exceeded everyone's gloomy expectations. For Poles, though, there was one huge consolation. For them the new pope was their primate! Glemp became almost irrelevant. For RFE he was a problem and an embarrassment. It was as polite as it could be.

In the second half of 1981 virtually the whole world, not just Poles, became first apprehensive and then fearful about the situation in Poland. Solidarity had ceased to be a trade union movement and had become a national movement. The Polish communist party had totally lost its authority. Authority in Poland had moved to Solidarity. Lech Wałęsa, the Solidarity leader, was a moderate in both methods and political ambitions, but was finding it increasingly difficult to control the less cautious elements nominally in his charge.

Certainly by the beginning of December a Soviet invasion was not just being feared, it was expected. Rumors out of Moscow itself were almost pinpointing the day. But the domestic military coup that actually occurred took everybody by surprise. The coup was led by General Wojciech Jaruzelski, who had recently risen up the

Polish power hierarchy to become communist Poland's virtual dictator. After the coup, carried out with astonishing precision and effectiveness, the communist party and the government practically disappeared. The Church, with Wyszyński dead, Pope John Paul II injured in Rome, and Glemp ineffective, was giving no leadership to society. Solidarity, too, almost at a stroke, had been forcibly submerged (although, as the future soon showed, by no means suppressed).

What those December days meant was that Radio Free Europe had more responsibility than ever before, and both Michałowski and I were aware of this. Extra care was now demanded. But a few members of the Polish Broadcast Service reacted differently. They were disappointed that the coup had been met with little overt resistance, that casualties had been almost unbelievably small.

The most serious incident was at the Wujek colliery near Katowice, where police killed between eleven and fifteen miners. A Reuters correspondent in Vienna made me aware of this in a matter of hours after this incident had occurred. I told Michałowski, and we agreed to keep silent for the moment. But very soon the news sped around the Polish Service, and an angry group of Polish editors confronted me, accusing me of suppressing the truth and demanding that the news be given full play. What they really wanted was to spread the news in the hope that it would arouse widespread resistance in Poland. (Obviously news of the Wujek killings had spread throughout Poland very soon after they occurred, often in a wildly exaggerated form. But there was no, or hardly any, active resistance).

I felt sorry for Michałowski during these difficult days. Breast-beating colleagues constantly confronted him, but the stubborn streak in his nature, which I had previously encountered from time to time, stood him, the Radio, and the Polish nation in good stead.

Communism Dying

Jaruzelski's coup was supposed to save communism in Poland. It finally killed it. It was really the Polish people who had been destroying it for over a quarter of a century by their character and resolution. Pope John Paul had given it the last rites on his first visit in 1979, and now Jaruzelski, its purported savior, dispatched it forever.

Mikhail Gorbachev conducted the funeral service when he renounced the "Brezhnev Doctrine," invoked by the Soviet regime to "justify" the invasion of Czechoslovakia. The deterrent that had helped to preserve communism in Eastern Europe was thus put aside. Now the popular will would decide. That being the case, communism had no chance. Jaruzelski seems to have realized this from the start. What he set up was a reformist military regime. It was an elaborate venture that grew increasingly absurd and pathetic throughout the 1980s. Now, looking at it, after an interval of twenty years, one is struck by how pathetic it was. The limitations of the military mind! After just a couple of years the Polish people were not groaning under it; they were laughing at it.

The fatal decline of communism in Eastern Europe occurred first in Poland. But its deathbed was already being prepared all over the region. In Hungary, Kádár was faltering, physically, mentally, and politically. The reforms he had begun were still sweeping on, less communist and more capitalist every day. Nothing of the sort was happening in Romania, of course, but Ceauşescu had been making his country virtually independent for years now. And with no Brezhnev Doctrine, the Soviets had openly to settle for it. In Czechoslovakia and the German Democratic Republic (GDR), the structure and formalities of communist power survived exasperatingly long. But Václav Havel, certainly not Gustáv Husák, was now the moral, and even the political, leader of most Czechs and Slovaks. And the GDR was clearly getting worried, not so much about the survival of "Socialism" but about the survival of itself. As for the Bulgarians, they patiently waited for another deliverance in their long history.

At the turn of the 1980s communism had ceased as a live force in Eastern Europe. Worse, it had become an irrelevance. Therefore it was dead. It would suffer the same in the Soviet Union, too, in just a few years. Gorbachev showed it could not survive even his own tinkering, let alone a transformation. Mankind was lucky, luckier still that it all happened with virtually no loss of life.

Radio Liberty's Hour

The Cold War was now essentially over in Eastern Europe. What

RFE needed now were "mopping-up" operations, not the mounting of new offensives. It was now Radio Liberty's hour. It still had real work to do. The Soviet Union in the early eighties looked decrepit but certainly not dead. It was only when Gorbachev tried to revive it that it died, without dignity but with all due speed.

Radio Liberty took its opportunity. I had the chance to read some of its scripts during the eighties and, like others who did the same, was struck by how good they were. RL Research, taking on new staff, produced some remarkable analyses, and its reputation markedly increased. The morale of the whole station rose. In short, Radio Liberty became a quality operation.

9

Alarums and Excursions

On the evening of February 21, 1981, my doorbell in Munich rang imperiously. A colleague was at the door telling me about a bomb at the Radio. I made the short drive to the Radio into pandemonium outside the building. The milling crowd forced me to park at least 200 yards away. The Munich police, calm as always, eventually gave me a pass to proceed further. Coming to the building I found most of the windows shattered and considerable damage to the wing that housed the Czechoslovak Broadcasting Service, including Czechoslovak News. The bomb, later estimated at up to 20 kgs, had injured three of the Czechoslovak news staff on duty: a woman who had her face damaged; a man who lost an eye; and another man whose hearing was permanently impaired.

Once in the building I arranged for all the Broadcast Services to put out an urgent news item on the blast and an assurance that normal broadcasting would go on. Then I went to the local hospital where the three injured Czechoslovaks were being treated. Then I went home.

The next day, a Sunday, the Radio was full. Staffers came out of loyalty, worry, curiosity, or helpfulness. I held a meeting with all five Broadcast Service directors and my deputy, Bob Hutchings, and we agreed that each Service should do a special brief broadcast about the bomb, telling what we knew and what we didn't know, namely, who had planted it. I left the directors to write their own programs and did not ask to see them before they were broadcast. I never read them. That was where trust came in. What struck me about the building on that Sunday morning were the calm and collegiality of the staff. It was no surprise to me; I had known most of them for many years. It was a heartwarming experience nonetheless.

Subsequently, though our first concern was for our injured colleagues, the paramount question was who did this. There were some wild suggestions, but for some time the hottest tip was a Czech, Pavel Minařík, who had worked in Munich at the Radio as an announcer for several years after the 1968 Soviet invasion of Czechoslovakia. He had then "redefected." Minařík indeed claimed for several years afterwards that he was the man behind the bomb but seemed to have difficulty in convincing anybody else that he was. He later appeared several times on Czechoslovak radio and television exposing the depravities of Radio Free Europe, occasionally joined by his Polish counterpart, Andrzej Czechowicz, who had returned to Poland in 1971. Later the situation became very misty. The East German Security Service (STASI) was alleged to have been involved, as was the Securitate, Romania's Security Service. The ubiquitous "classic terrorist" Carlos was also said to be implicated, and there was much speculation about his alleged involvement.[5] Whoever or whatever it was, it marked the serious beginning of the "wet work" phase in the East's campaign against Radio Free Europe. "Wet work," I later learnt from security cognoscenti, meant deeds involving blood-spilling. RFE's response was to build protective walls and insert double-glazed windows. We were all told to be on the "lookout" but also to "keep calm."

"Redefectors"

Czechowicz, the Pole, had been a junior researcher in the Polish section of the Research and Analysis Department. I got to know him slightly and had rather liked him. I always found it hard to believe that he was the "ace of intelligence" Radio Warsaw later made him out to be. In one of his interviews in Warsaw he described me as a "CIA colonel," a much higher rank than I ever had with the Royal Air Force.

I sometimes even wondered whether Czechowicz did come to RFE as a ready-made spy or whether he gradually became one in exile—a country lad, homesick, or disaffected with the Radio, perhaps hard up for money, then befriended by one of the numerous Eastern agents working in West Germany, and eventually induced to go back home as an "ace of intelligence" with as much incriminating material as he could lay his hands on. In the event, he did Radio Free Europe little or no harm. Rather, he made a fool of himself in Poland, despised even by many communists there.[6]

Not long after Czechowicz, a Polish married couple redefected. He also worked in Polish Research, she in Monitoring. They were always rather a sad pair and were reportedly even sadder when they got home.

There was no doubt that various kinds of communist pressure, direct or indirect, were put on RFE's exiles either to pass on information (once they did this, of course, they were hooked), become full agents for the East European security services, or just return home. On several occasions over the years, some of my exile colleagues showed me letters purportedly written by mothers or fathers imploring them to return. The Radio's Security Department was kept busy by such letters. More important, it was also kept busy by some serious incidents affecting RFE members, especially during the last years of the Cold War.

Murder: Attempted and Suspected

On a summer morning in July 1981 I got a call in my office from the wife of Emil Georgescu, one of the top Romanian Service editors. Mrs. Georgescu was totally hysterical. Two men had stabbed her husband several times outside their home. I got in touch immediately with Rich Cummings, the security director, who drove out to the Georgescu's home and duly confirmed that an attempt had been made to murder him and had very nearly succeeded. Two low-level French criminals were involved and were soon taken in. Georgescu was taken to hospital, the police were called in, and back at RFE I tried to calm a panic-stricken clutch of the Radio's Romanian staff. After consulting with Cummings and others I tried to quiet them by saying that Georgescu may have been attacked not for his RFE broadcasts, but for certain "shady dealings" he was alleged to have had in the local Munich underworld. I was sincere in saying this, but it was thoroughly unconvincing and certainly did not calm the Romanian staff.

Emil Georgescu was a brilliant broadcaster but an unsavory character. He had been a Bucharest city prosecutor before fleeing to the West and had been snapped up by Noel Bernard on the strength of his intimate knowledge of the inadequacies of Romanian Communist law, in theory and in practice. He soon acquired a huge audience. Apparently he also rattled Ceaușescu personally. Time for action, therefore, against this renegade shyster! Time for wet work!

Georgescu survived, recovered, and returned to work at the Radio, although he was never the same again and died soon afterwards. But he was not the only RFE Romanian celebrity to die during these febrile years. Noel Bernard himself had died of lung cancer some time before the Georgescu incident. Mihai ("Mike") Cismarescu, his successor as Romanian director, died of stomach cancer, and then Cismarescu's successor, Vlad Georgescu, a noted scholar and former political prisoner under Ceaușescu, died of a malignant brain tumor. No Romanian anywhere, certainly not in Radio Free Europe, would believe that this was all coincidence. They were convinced of a diabolical threefold murder, and their certainties were subsequently confirmed by Ion Mihai Pacepa, a former top official in the Romanian Securitate coterie close to Ceaușescu himself. Pacepa defected to the United States in 1978 and "told all."

The trouble was that Pacepa had been a liar all his life and obviously did not discover truth when he landed in America. He was soon dismissed by all who met him there as a thoroughly unreliable character. Pacepa gave chapter and verse for what he called the deliberately induced cancers that killed Bernard, Cismarescu, and Vlad Georgescu, but all the qualified medical opinion that was consulted simply rejected this notion as impossible.

These three deaths as well as the Pacepa revelations certainly seemed to indicate that the "wet work" was flowing. The question was how much. A proneness to paranoia and *folie des grandeurs* obviously existed in exile organizations like Radio Free Europe. For example, some telephones were indeed being tapped, but many more were *believed* to be. Some apartments were entered illegally, but many more were *said* to have been entered illegally. When I was deputy director at the Radio in the 1970s, one Bulgarian editor was truly convinced that he was being followed daily. A "Politburo decision" had set this in motion, he said. Eventually he agreed to take psychiatric help.

The Markov Murder

All the same, there can be no question that, as the communist system began unraveling, some of its leaders became ready for mayhem. The most sinister such case was the killing of the exile Bulgarian writer, Georgi Markov, in London. Markov escaped from Bulgaria in the summer of 1969. In 1975, he agreed to do some free-lance programming with RFE's Bulgarian Service. The most notable of his scripts was a series called "Meetings with Todor Zhivkov," eleven of them.[7] Along with other writers Markov had periodically met Zhivkov before he defected, and they seem to have chatted informally with him. (This was when Zhivkov was going through a "cultural phase." See his letter to the Writers' Union chief mentioned in chapter 6.)

Markov's scripts about Zhivkov were skittishly critical but hardly insulting by any Western democratic standards. What emerged from the scripts was essentially a decent man spoiled by power and pretension. The Bulgarian Service director, Metodi Zaharieff, consulted me about the scripts before broadcasting them. To be certain, I got all of them fully translated. They struck me, as they also struck Zaharieff, as quality material. But suitable for broadcasting? Zaharieff thought they were and, after much reflection, so did I. To make sure, I asked one of my colleagues, a mature Scot, to read them, too. He agreed with our view but pointed to one script, in which Markov had a bit of fun about Zhivkov's signature, as perhaps questionable. I told Zaharieff to go ahead with that one, too.

Sometime afterwards, on September 7, 1978, Markov was stabbed in the calf with a poisoned umbrella point on Waterloo Bridge in London. He died on September 11, 1978. His stab wound contained a dose of Ricin, a highly toxic poison. The murder caused an international commotion in which RFE and the BBC naturally figured. (The BBC, as always, was cooperative and reasonable.) The commotion blew over but I naturally asked myself whether I should have authorized those scripts. I decided I had been right. Markov knew what he was doing and had evidently been threatened by Bulgarian regime agents several times before. The grieving of his lovely wife, though, gave me much pause for thought afterwards.

10

The Sea Change

The sea change came in 1980 with Ronald Reagan's victory at the presidential polls. The world changed, and so did Radio Free Europe. The change had been coming ever since 1964 when Barry Goldwater got over 26 million votes in the presidential election, nowhere near enough to touch Lyndon Johnson but not bad for a "conservative" Republican. An American friend told me just two years later that the United States was a "deeply conservative country." I only realized how conservative after 1980. In 1957 when I joined RFE, liberalism was an American dynamic. When I left it in 1983, it had become a fading American tradition and a dirty word in much of American society. As for "moderate Republicans" they had become a dying sect.

I should have seen it coming. But cocooned in my Munich haven, visiting America often but usually not for long enough, I didn't. I knew there would be changes but didn't fully grasp their significance. I worked for Radio Free *Europe*, and for nearly a quarter of a century its European orientation had been encouraged. But the days of "European-ness" were over. This was soon spelled out to me by a self-confident young member of the RFE/RL "transition team" sent from Washington after Reagan's victory in November 1980. RFE/RL was "an American radio station and nobody had better forget it."

The change was in people, programs, and philosophy. But looking back it didn't much matter for Radio Free Europe. As I have argued in chapter 8, communism was beaten in Eastern Europe by 1981. There the Cold War had already been won, not by Radio Free Europe, of course, but by the East European people. Communism was lost in its own vicious incompetence and historic irrelevance.

The New Brooms

I remained at the Radio long enough to see how the Reagan Revolution was affecting it. I remember at the time, despite my forebodings, being anxious to stay. Looking back it would have been better, more honest, to have resigned immediately.

President Reagan appointed Frank Shakespeare as the new BIB chairman. "Something had to be found for a true believer like Frank," as one Washington insider put it to me. He had first made his presence felt as Nixon's head of the United States Information Agency (USIA), a presence that now apparently made his absence from anything like senior office imperative. I had met Frank Shakespeare several times in Munich, twice during the transitional period after November 1980 and then at a crucial meeting in Washington. I was summoned to this meeting in February 1981 at very short notice. Also present were Ben Wattenberg, his newly appointed Democratic deputy at the BIB, and George Bailey, about to be anointed director of Radio Liberty. I had met Wattenberg earlier during the transitional period. Bailey I had met years before when he had come to RFE in Munich to do a story for the old *Reporter* magazine. I also knew of his high reputation as a journalist and linguist.

The meeting in Washington was brief. Shakespeare simply told us that he was firing Glenn Ferguson, the overall president of RFE/RL, and the long-serving Ralph Walter. He was retaining me at RFE and bringing Bailey in as RL director. After that it was the next plane back to Munich and rumor-rife RFE.

Frank Shakespeare was *sui generis*. He saw RFE/RL as his ideological toy, and he was bent on playing with it. He took pride in calling himself a "conservative's conservative." He was also a Mass-a-day Roman Catholic and an erstwhile president of the Heritage Foundation. Like many other Reagan revolutionaries he had a remarkable self-confidence; doubt never appeared on his radar. But there was nothing arrogant or brusque about him; he was affable enough, courteous even. Even so, he openly regarded America not just as God's own country but as God's only country. The RFE/RL staff in Munich he paternally regarded as benighted "outlanders," not just needing enlightenment but actually pining for it. I remember a fifteen-minute impromptu sermon of his on "supply-side economics" at a Christmas Party in Munich. It did little for the festive spirit and may even have converted a few of his bemused listeners to socialism.

Ben Wattenberg, the new BIB vice chairman, was a broadcaster by profession. He later became notable at the end of the Cold War for a remarkable series of patriotic outbursts about the greatness of America. I was working for Rand/UCLA at the time and they reminded me strongly of Dodgers' coach Tommy La Sorda's passionate variations on "America the Beautiful." Wattenberg sometimes felt that Shakespeare needed a bit of explaining. But the best I ever heard him come up with was: "Frank's always up front."

Just a word about Jim Buckley, whom Shakespeare appointed president of RFE/RL in Munich. For a relatively short time Buckley (known by some as the "nice Buckley," to distinguish him from his more famous sibling, Bill) had been a Republican senator for New York. He was also the first senator publicly to call for Nixon's resignation. More recently he had served as counselor in the State Department. Jim Buckley was a gentleman of a rather high order and earned respect, even esteem, during his short stay in Munich.

George Urban: Colleague and Successor

Shakespeare appointed George Urban RFE director almost immediately after I resigned. George and I had been good friends for over twenty years. In the mid-seventies he had suggested to me that RFE should begin a "University of the Air" series of programs. Each series should have a broad theme, and every program in a series should consist of Urban interviewing a distinguished expert on the subject. I responded eagerly, and we sold the idea to Ralph Walter, then director of Radio Free Europe. George had had a checkered career since first leaving the Radio in the early 1960s. This included relatively brief spells at Indiana University and the University of Southern California. He was then living in Brighton in England.

It soon became evident that high-class interviewing was George Urban's metier. His intellectual brilliance shone through in these "University of the Air" interviews. He worked hard preparing them, and in some he performed more impressively than his distinguished guest. Most of his guests were intellectuals, many of them world famous. Some of his interviews became better known through being published in *Encounter* in London, and then in book form. The interviewees included men like Ignazio Silone, Arthur Koestler, George Kennan, Raymond Aron, Milovan Djilas, Edward Heath, and many others of similar renown. The themes covered included the environment, détente, the role of universities, and various notions of Europe and of science in society. My job was the less glamorous one of finding enough RFE funds to keep Urban's interviews going. "Urban provides the brains, Brown the wherewithal." This was the way several of our colleagues summed up our partnership.

The "University of the Air" was an undoubted intellectual success. Whether it was a broadcasting success was more debatable. The interviews had to be translated from English into the "RFE languages." They also had to be condensed. Sometimes the quality of neither translation nor condensation was very high. The reaction of the Broadcast Services was mixed. Szabados of the Hungarian Service was enthusiastic and found the men and the means to get the interviews on the air in style. One service was decisively less enthusiastic and was eventually excused from carrying them. Two others complied but hardly cooperated. Still, the "University of the Air" had a small, slightly growing audience. I was not discouraged by the size of the audience. They were all heavyweights; perhaps not political heavyweights but life's heavyweights.

When his RFE career was finally over George wrote a book bent on vindicating it.[8] Though hardly an "Apologia pro Vita Sua," it was a spirited attempt at self-defense. Its theme can be summed up in a few words: RFE was going to the dogs before he took over and resumed its downward trajectory when he left.

Urban fully subscribed to Shakespeare's views about RFE's role in the Cold War. He was by no means the only brilliant intellectual who climbed on the Reagan bandwagon in 1980. He had never actually hidden his views before then, but rather veiled them.

Certainly his "University of the Air" interview programs, with the possible exception of the Détente series, were politically neutral. But he had to wait till Shakespeare's arrival before he found his political soul mate and could jettison his previous caution.

In retrospect, though, there was one thing rather odd or inconsistent about George Urban's appointment, and about George Bailey's, too. One of the key aspects of the Reagan "revolution" at RFE and RL was "re-Americanization." As I have already admitted, there was certainly some sense in the long-standing criticism, at least of RFE, that it had over the years become "too European." High time, therefore, to move it back across the Atlantic. Yet both Urban and Bailey were Hungarian-born. Urban was quite self-consciously the Central European intellectual, par excellence. Bailey had lived in continental Europe since the end of World War II and Urban in England for about the same period. Urban, I knew from personal experience, had little knowledge of America, less sympathy, and no empathy. It seems therefore that what attracted Shakespeare to them was less their cultural orientation than their ideology, their Manichean worldview. (Any suspicion that Frank might have been a secret internationalist could be dismissed out of hand.) In this they were truly his people.

George Urban certainly had his supporters at the Radio; they considered his hard line right and long overdue. There were, indeed, some imaginative strokes on his part. He was instrumental in getting broadcasting to the three Baltic republics—Estonia, Latvia, and Lithuania—taken from Radio Liberty and put under RFE. In some ways a new broom was needed, and he supplied it. He undoubtedly thought "big" and he "shook the place up." I, and perhaps other RFE "veterans," had allowed ourselves to get dragged too deeply into an administrative routine. We needed to be "shook up" too, perhaps "shook out" in one or two cases.

But what was truly significant about the Shakespeare-Urban "revolution" was that it was actually a "restoration"—a restoration of the philosophy, ethos, politics, and policies of the Radio in the 1950s before the Hungarian Revolution. Virtually everything that had happened at the Radio in the quarter century between 1956 and 1981 was now dismissed as having not been "anticommunist enough" or being "too soft on communism." RFE's debacle in the

Hungarian Revolution, it was now alleged, had in fact weakened RFE's anticommunist resolve. An executive of RFE in New York told me in December 1980 that Shakespeare was convinced that there was "something fundamentally wrong with the Radio's politics." With attitudes like this, it was not surprising that the RFE of the 1980s soon began to look more than ever like the RFE of the 1950s. Nor was it just a question of programming substance: the presentation changed too. The gloves were off; it was back to bare knuckles.

11

People and Memories

I resigned from Radio Free Europe early in 1983, a move that I and others had long known was inevitable. As often in such a situation the specific reason for resignation was relatively trivial. Shakespeare was determined to appoint someone as the new director of the Czechoslovak Service whom I thought totally unsuitable. But had I not resigned then, I would have been dismissed almost any time later. The new RFE and I were just not compatible. Shortly before I took the decision, I got a postcard from Bill Griffith at MIT. "Hold the fort," was his message. But the Beau Geste days were over. The time before finally leaving Munich was stressful, eased only by the support of my wife, daughters, and good friends, and the considerateness of Jim Buckley, now in his own last phase at the Radio.

Back in England after nearly thirty years I began writing books for Duke University Press, became a Senior Research Associate at St Antony's College in Oxford, and had seven happy years of university teaching in places as far flung as Berkeley, Berlin, and Bulgaria.

But Radio Free Europe has remained my life experience, the orbit around which my life has always revolved, the place to which my thoughts have continued to return. Perhaps this memoir will help me get RFE out of my system. What remains most strongly with me is the feel, the character, the ambience of the place. I will, therefore, devote my last few pages trying to explain, or illustrate, what I mean.

RFE was a pressure cooker that never exploded because at certain crucial times there were leaders who kept calm and kept everybody else calm, and who kept control firmly, fairly, and judiciously. Occasionally there was serious dissension in all the Broadcast Services. But there was little of the chronic "way-of-life" strife that characterized many exile organizations.

This was because, in spite of its "European-ness," Radio Free Europe was indeed, an *American* organization, and not just an *American-run* organization. To RFE's exile staff America became an ideal, hope, and sanctuary. They were sometimes bemused and bewildered by it, but they trusted it. And while for most of them America was not their only available recourse, it was their *best* recourse. America, therefore, their trust in it and unity behind it, transcended their national jealousies and workplace resentments. I once remember a Bulgarian colleague who was just resuming work in Munich after finally getting his U.S. citizenship. There were tears in his eyes as he showed me his new passport. At last he was *in*!

Experiences like this brought home to me the human quality of the Radio, and they refresh and illuminate my memories of it. It was this human quality that nurtured the enjoyment, fun even, that pervaded so much of my experience of it. Talking about "fun" may seem a pretty knock-about way of ending a memoir about an organization whose aim was so serious. But I make no apologies for it. I recall Montaigne, himself a man of underlying seriousness, writing somewhere that "wisdom should have a madcap quality" about it. There was certainly a "madcap quality" about RFE, not so much in its work as in its unwinding. Two examples out of many, spring to mind.

For three years the Polish Service held an annual "Bastard of the Year" competition. (No prizes.) Then they gave it up because the same man won it three years in a row and was still a long way from retirement. Then there was Rosi, a traditionally built, elderly Bavarian waitress in the canteen who invariably addressed Zygmunt Michałowski, the Polish Service director in the late seventies, as "Herr Geheimrat" (Privy Councilor). Nobody, including Michałowski, had any idea why. Rosi herself never let on why. (Michałowski was secretly flattered.)

Then there was the plentiful supply of RFE "characters." I shall recall just two.

Count Kajetan Czarkowski-Golujewski was a Habsburg Polish aristocrat. When I came to the Radio in 1957, he was already there as head of the Polish Research Section, a post for which, as he himself would cheerfully admit, he was manifestly unsuited. Later he joined the Radio's Public Relations Department, "putting him out of harm's way," as someone surmised. His job there was to take tours of visitors round the building. His easy irreverence about the Radio bemused some visitors. But his unfailing courtesy and equability charmed everyone. Every tour a hit!

Czarkowski, the classic "toff," was totally without snobbery. He married while at the Radio. His wife Klara, a Hungarian lady from the Károlyi family, worked as a typist at the Radio. Another "toff," she was also totally without snobbery, and like him, she effortlessly exuded "quality." During World War I Czarkowski flew warplanes for Austria-Hungary and was decorated for bombing Venice. "Hand-job," he assured everybody. "They all fell into the lagoon." In the interwar period he tried flying around the world, crashed in Burma, and lost an eye. He wore a glass eye in its place, which he enjoyed identifying in company by tapping it firmly with a biro pen. He cheated his way through his German driving test by a whirling movement of his arms. Not surprisingly, he was one of the worst drivers in the entire Radio.

Czarkowski dressed "English," which meant Harris Tweed jackets, cavalry twills, and "brothel-creeper" suede shoes. In winter he wore a Lodenfrei overcoat and an expensive green Alpine hat. He spoke excellent English and several other European languages. He had a pleasant voice but a disconcerting "Basil Brush" type laugh. He was a much-loved man. Just to see him on the corridor was an assurance.

RFE's greatest comic character was undoubtedly Ion Gheorghe, head of Romanian Research for nearly thirty years. Gheorghe's father had been the last Romanian ambassador to Nazi Germany. Mr. Gheorghe himself (it was nearly always *Mr.* Gheorghe) never betrayed his political convictions, but he was clearly no liberal. Like many comic characters he took himself very seriously. He was also remarkably intelligent, knowledgeable, and diligent. But it was his personality that immortalized him. His niggardliness was notorious. He ate next to nothing and drank only coffee and

Fanta. Yet it was Mr. Gheorghe who, all passion spent after one of our frequent arguments, would sometimes say, "You know, Mr. Brown, this is the kind of discussion we should have over brandy and cigars."

His clothes were patchy and gamy. Yet he was a very rich man, gossip having it that when he visited his local bank, the genuflecting manager appeared as if from nowhere. Then, one day in the summer of 1973, he showed his unsuspected thespian touch. He appeared in my office in a brand new suit, Sears Roebuck true, but Savile Row compared with his previous wardrobe. Next, within a couple of days, Mr. Gheorghe had jettisoned his pre–World War II bicycle (about which the Munich police had warned him several times), and drove into RFE's car park in a late-fifties Cadillac, of blinding color and with fins at their apogee. Once in the office the first thing he did every morning was to feed the pigeons on his windowsill. His office was almost surreal in its messiness.

He conducted a protracted feud with Central News. In the mid-seventies the Central News introduced a brief fortnightly press release on developments in Eastern Europe. It was transmitted to news agencies and newspapers in the West and got good usage. But there was always one snag—Mr. Gheorghe. The Central News depended on the five research sections to provide it with the necessary information and sometimes suggestions on subjects to cover. To simplify matters it sent out fortnightly questionnaires to each section. The responses from the Bulgarian, Polish, Hungarian, and Czechoslovak sections were generally helpful. But from the Romanian (Mr. Gheorghe's) section, the answers were invariable: "We have no informations (sic) on this subject in our files."

The News Room was at first puzzled, and then it bridled. Late one night two of its editors ambushed Mr. Gheorghe on one of his frequent news-hungry visits to the News Room and barred his exit. Then, perhaps not as politely as they could, they expressed their profound dissatisfaction and rather forlornly appealed to Mr. Gheorghe's corporate spirit. Mr. Gheorghe's excuse seems to have centered on his staff shortages and what he considered the obscure nature of some of the themes covered in the questionnaires.

"OK, Mr. Gheorghe, why don't *you* suggest a theme"? Mr. Gheorghe then muttered something about nuclear energy in Eastern

Europe. "Right on, Mr. Gheorghe, brilliant idea!" came the response. The questionnaire was duly prepared, purposefully simplified, and sent down to the Research Sections. In a few days their responses drifted back. From the Bulgarians, Poles, Czechoslovaks, and Hungarians, it was the usual competent effort. From Mr. Gheorghe it was "We have no informations on this subject in our files."

Mr. Gheorghe may never have drunk, but there were very few teetotalers at RFE. Jack Anderson, with his characteristic blend of prejudice and pith, once characterized the Radio as being "awash with booze." Some of our wives may sometimes have agreed with him. Sex also occasionally reared its ugly head; but, fortunately or unfortunately, RFE was never the pullulating bordello the communist press made it out to be.

Finally, a very personal note. In 1992 I was in the Prague Castle being introduced, along with many others, to President Václav Havel. I was introduced as a former director of Radio Free Europe. Havel looked at me, smiled, and said "Jim! We were colleagues!" That made everything worthwhile.

Epilogue:

Over Too Soon

The Cold war was over in Eastern Europe by 1989, an ending as momentous as it was unexpected.

But what then? Obviously it would be absurd to say that winning the Cold War was the "easy part" for Radio Free Europe, and now the "hard part" was just beginning. But as I have argued in this book, RFE had a dual task—fighting both *against* communism and *for* democracy. So it now became evident that the second part of RFE's dual purpose needed to be brought exclusively into play.

Radio Free Europe, therefore, should not only have been continued but also transformed. And that transformation should have begun in the late 1980s when it was obvious that communism in Eastern Europe was in rapid, terminal decay. The same applied to Radio Liberty; very soon the first part of *its* dual task would be over and the second part, much more complex and difficult, would need to begin.

The transformation was never begun because American opinion, official and public, held that with the defeat of communism no further struggle was needed. Democracy, it was assumed, had already triumphed, and capitalism, "its essential concomitant," would soon begin transforming the economies of Eastern Europe into efficient vehicles of prosperity. I lived in the United States for several years during and after the fall of communism in Eastern Europe and was almost unnerved by the triumphalist self-congratulation pervading public life there.

In practical terms Radio Free Europe became the victim of the clamor for the "peace dividend." It was seen as no longer necessary and was costing too much anyway. One or two senators and several representatives chose to make an issue out of the burgeoning costs of the Munich operation and the occasional wastefulness of the RFE/RL leadership. In the national mood of "Cold War won," any argument that there was still much to do fell on deaf ears. And the revelations of how expensive the Cold Warriors were alleged to be only strengthened the feeling in Washington of job well done, red devil gone, now let's get back to counting the pennies.

What soon became certain was that both Radios, on account of costs, would have to get out of Munich. The German government would have eventually wanted them out, too. But the euphoria and distractions over reunification and the new mood of gratitude to America, however temporary, would have given the Radios freedom to stay in Munich at least till the end of the Millennium. But in the early nineties, President Václav Havel made his noble offer of hospitality: RFE/RL should move into the former Czechoslovak parliament building in Prague, now surplus to requirements since the breakup of Czechoslovakia. It was an offer no one could refuse, and it probably saved RFE from total extinction. As it was, broadcasting to Hungary, Poland, the new Czech Republic, and the new Slovakia soon ceased after the move to Prague. Some broadcasting to Romania and Bulgaria continued for a while, and new services were sensibly established for the Balkans.[9] But in spite of these welcome additions Radio Free Europe became a mere shell of its former self.

The Need for Munich

Without wishing to detract from Havel's generosity in granting RFE/RL the asylum it needed, it must still be emphasized that the stations should have been enabled to stay in Munich. Prague was not the place for Radio Free Europe to continue its mission. That place was Munich; not just because it had always been there, although continuity of location was unquestionably important. The most important reason was that Munich was not in Eastern Europe, whereas Prague was still in "Eastern Europe," at least till the political and ideological maps finally changed. Non-Czech listeners would not have remained faithful listeners to a Prague-based RFE. With Radio Liberty it would have been quite different. Its Russian, Belarusian, and Ukrainian listeners were not much affected by the move to Prague, its Asian listeners not at all.

Had RFE been maintained as a meaningful post–Cold War broadcaster it would inevitably have become different from what it had once been. First, it could have been much smaller, requiring less than half its previous staff. This was mainly because its broadcasting time could have been drastically reduced, from say seventeen hours a day to Poland to six hours a day. To Hungary it could even have dropped to five hours daily, for the Czech Republic and Slovakia three each, and the same for Bulgaria and Romania. The savings involved here would have been significant, perhaps not significant enough for those in Washington determined to close the Radio, but perhaps persuasive enough for the more far-sighted politicians to remain open to the argument that "Eastern Europe" still needed attention, if of a new kind. What it needed now was similar treatment to that which Western Europe got from America after World War II. That treatment was predicated on the realization that defeating Nazi Germany militarily was only the *first* phase. In 1945, though the war might be over, the peace had now to be won. So in 1989 the Cold War was over, but the peace was not won.

The EU: Roles and Responsibilities

Obviously it was Western Europe, through the European Union, that had now to shoulder most of the responsibility—economic, political, and social—for the resuscitation of Eastern Europe. But America was crucial, too, and not only because of its unchallenged strength. America was indissolubly linked with Eastern Europe through more than a century of migration. Between the end of the American Civil War in 1865 and the beginning of World War I, America became the land of hope not only for the millions of East Europeans who actually emigrated there but also for the millions of their relatives who stayed behind, remaining in close touch with those who had emigrated, and often envying them too. America remained their hope, too, during the Cold War, and now was

America's chance to fulfill its historic mission. RFE could certainly have helped by continuing to be a powerful symbol of American concern.

Radio New Europe

And the cost? Jan Nowak used to be fond of saying that Radio Free Europe cost less than one part of a U.S. fighter airplane. The comparison was still worth keeping in mind. Radio Free Europe could have become Radio New Europe, doing different but just as essential work. And cheap at the price! There was room for America, and certainly the need for America, in the new Eastern Europe.

America would have to have been the *lesser* of two partners: the dominant role had to be the European Union's. But would America, now the only superpower, have been prepared to play second fiddle in *any* orchestra, playing any composition, however uplifting? Many Americans would have found this psychologically impossible. But at the same time many of those same Americans had for years been demanding that Western Europe should "pay its share" and assume responsibilities commensurate with its growing wealth and in keeping with the geopolitics of Europe. Certainly for most East Europeans a reorganized Radio *New* Europe, still at least partly American financed and American-led, would have been powerful evidence of Washington's continuing commitment to their region.

Explaining Democracy

In his wonderful book *Black Sea*, Neal Ascherson talks to a historian, a lady who was also for a time the Abkhazian minister of information. The year was 1993. "In the Brezhnev days," she told him, "I was one of those who listened to Radio Liberty and thought that democracy would be such a natural, simple thing. Now I realize that in real life matters are much more difficult." What went for Abkhazia certainly went for Eastern Europe. Radio New Europe could have helped in explaining the workings, difficulties, complexities, and varieties, the successes and failures so far, of democracy. True, immediately after the end of the Cold War it did seem for a short time that democracy (like capitalism) was "busting out all over" in Eastern Europe. Easy! Freedom of speech sprang into life. So did freedom of association and movement. So did a bewildering number of newspapers and magazines (*Dilemma Review*, Bucharest, was my favorite.)

Nongovernmental organizations (NGOs) sprouted everywhere. Parliamentary and local elections, hotly contested, took place. It all seemed that the necessary leap into the democratic arena had indeed been made. But, everybody was deceived, most of all the East Europeans. These early flurries were not making democracy; they were detracting from its essential requirements. As I argued in my book *The Grooves of Change: Eastern Europe at the Turn of the Millennium* (Duke University Press, 2001), these requirements were: minimum level of material standards; civil society and the growth of a civic class; an evolving political culture; and the growth of a civil statism reflected in the characteristics of a legal state.

These requirements have not yet been met anywhere in the former Soviet Union except in the Baltic Republics. Ukraine and Georgia, despite their encouraging turns, still remain question marks.

And, for several years after 1989, they were not being satisfactorily met in most of the former East European satellites either. In Poland, for example, Lech Wałęsa, one of the Cold War's true heroes, showed himself to be no devotee of free elections when he lost them. In Slovakia Vladimír Mečiar had more in common with that Belarusian political freak Alexander Lukashenko than any other living political figure. And Mečiar had widespread political support for far too long. In Hungary irredentism came close to the political surface, and a sometimes aggressive nationalism became a permanent fixture. As for Romania and Bulgaria, they remained still the furthest away from even the minimum democratic standards.

Therefore, what the former components of the Soviet Union dangerously had and what its former East European satellites suspiciously had was not democracy but various forms of what became called, *demokratura*: democratic forms but neither democratic substance nor democratic spirit. And behind these democratic forms a depressing postcommunist system was developing, characterized by multilevel corruption, fraudulent elections, and ubiquitous gangsterism. Its populations were dividing between those on upward escalators carrying "a mix of opportunist former apparatchiks and talented, flexible-minded youth and those on downward escalators carrying virtually everybody else—dazed, resentful, and nostalgic for the remembered security of the old regime." Finally, in the former Yugoslavia there was the worst ethnic slaughter Europe had seen since World War II. Milošević and company were but the foulest excrescences of the old *nomenklatura*.

What pulled Eastern Europe from this downward path was the European Union—the prospect of joining it and, crucially, the requirements for joining it. These requirements were all-embracing, penetrating every branch in the applicants' public life. And they were strictly enforced. Now Estonia, Latvia, Lithuania, Poland, the Czech Republic, Slovakia, Hungary, and Slovenia are EU members. By 2010 Bulgaria and Romania should be also. Macedonia, Albania, Serbia, and Bosnia must wait longer, perhaps much longer.[10]

What part could "Radio New Europe" have played in this historic development? Very little, relatively; but still something very much worth doing. It could have incessantly stressed the differences between *demokratura* and real democracy. It could have run daily cross-reporting programs on *real* democratic progress in individual East European countries, interviewing leading politicians and intellectuals in the region, interviewing "ordinary" people too about what they thought and what was worrying them. Reaching out to the *ordinary* people was crucial. There were too many philosopher kings in postcommunist Eastern Europe. Some of them needed quickly dethroning.

Another valuable service would have been a daily or thrice-weekly West European and American press review. East European audiences wanted to know, and needed to know, what the rest of the world was doing, thinking, and saying about them. And it is worth remembering that the European Union had no radio station of its own. Nor did NATO for that matter.

Nor was it only politics and economics that were of vital concern. Numerous social issues needed exploring and explaining—the whole Roma issue, for example, the harrowing conditions in Romania's orphanages, and so on. Radio New Europe could have offered a whole bill or fare, compelling and enlightening.

But Radio New Europe never came about. Radio Free Europe is deservedly remembered, but it need not have petered out when it did and the way it did. There was still much for it to do, many services for it to perform. Its real job was only half-done.

Notes

Added by A. Ross Johnson

1. Some jamming of RFE Polish broadcasts continued from the USSR.
2. Khrushchev's so-called "Secret Speech" was delivered on February 25, 1956, and broadcast by RFE after publication in *The New York Times* in June.
3. RFE broadcast briefly to Albania in 1950–1951.
4. RFE/RL inaugurated broadcasts to former Yugoslavia in 1994.
5. It was later established that the Carlos group had carried out the bombing for Ceauşescu (Richard H. Cummings, *Cold War Radio; The Dangerous History of American Broadcasting in Europe, 1950–1989* [Jefferson, NC: McFarland, 2009], Chapter 4, "Carlos the Jackal and the Bombing of Radio Free Europe/Radio Liberty").
6. Paweł Machcewicz later provided detailed analysis of the Czechowicz case based on Polish regime archives ("Polish Regime Countermeasures Against Radio Free Europe," in A. Ross Johnson and R. Eugene Parta, eds, *Cold War Broadcasting; Impact on the Soviet Union and Eastern Europe* [Budapest: Central European University Press, 2010]).
7. The translated series was later published in Georgi Markov, *The Truth That Killed* (New York: Ticknor & Fields, 1984), pp. 215–63).
8. George R. Urban, *Radio Free Europe and the Pursuit of Democracy: My War within the Cold War* (New Haven: Yale University Press, 1997).
9. RFE broadcasts to Hungary ended in 1993, to Poland (from Warsaw) in 1997, to the Czech Republic (in partnership with Czech Public Radio after 1994) in 2002, to Slovakia, Bulgaria, Estonia, Latvia, and Lithuania in 2004, and to Romania in 2008. Broadcasts to former Yugoslavia began in 1994.
10. Bulgaria and Romania joined the EU in 2007. Croatia joined in 2013.

Index

www.ingramcontent.com/pod-product-compliance
Lightning Source LLC
Chambersburg PA
CBHW020614270326
41927CB00005B/329